The Honest Real Estate Agent

ISBN: 1-4792-1339-X
ISBN-13: 9781479213399

The Honest Real Estate Agent

A Training Guide for a Successful First Year and Beyond as a Real Estate Agent

Mario Jannatpour

2012

Dedication

I dedicate this book to my parents, Kaz and Virginia Jannatpour. I love you both for all the sacrifices and hard work you did for our family while we were growing up. I am glad you both had the courage to come to the United States so you could meet and then myself and my two brothers could be alive today. Thank you for everything.

Table of Contents

Acknowledgements

I would like to thank the following people for their help, advice and support during my journey of writing this book.

First, I want to thank Amanda Warton Jenkins for her awesome work and enthusiasm in editing the book. I am so lucky to know Amanda because she is amazing with the English language and is a great salesperson in her own right.

A special thanks and tip of the hat to Addy Saeed, Jeff Rising and Larry Lawfer: three of my Realtor friends who encouraged and supported me to write another book on being a real estate agent. All three are very special people and I am so happy they are my friends now.

Thank you to Jennifer Allan-Hagedorn for reading the book and offering her feedback to help make the book a little bit better. I really appreciate Jennifer taking the time to help me out.

I want to thank the following Realtors for sharing their stories with me to include in this book: Michael James, Liz Caraway, Andrea Martone, Jean Griswold, Loretta Jobs, Richie Alan Naggar, Susan Plage, and Margaret Woda.

All of the Realtors who helped me with my book are very successful and they are truly honest with their clients, their business and themselves. Their contributions to this book make it very special.

I want to thank all of my Facebook friends and family who contributed their thoughts and opinions concerning real estate agents. The consumer feedback I received from my Facebook friends set me on my path to coming up with the title of the book and seeing the truth to the heart of the message in this book.

Thanks to Greg Jenkins for his help and expertise with my business. Greg is a great sounding board for me and is always there when I need to talk to someone. He probably thinks I am crazy for wanting to continue writing books, and that's what I like about him; he see things differently than I do.

Thanks to all of my past clients and future clients. I have the best job in the world as a real estate agent because I get to work with such great people, and my clients do a great job of keeping me honest.

Thank you to Ryan Higgens for his amazing help in proofreading and suggesting final edits. His assistance was invaluable. I wish Ryan good luck in his new career as a Realtor in the Boston area.

The BIGGEST and MOST IMPORTANT thank you goes out to my wife, Smitha, and our two daughters, Ria and Puja. I am a lucky man to have such a great family. My three girls keep me grounded and don't let any of this book stuff go to my head.

Introduction

Some people in the book publishing business say that when you write a book you should come up with the title before writing it. That is easier said than done. I had a hard time trying to come up with a title for this book. I had a lot of ideas and thoughts for a title and here are some of them:

- **The Smart Real Estate Agent**
- **The Rich Real Estate Agent**
- **The Savvy Real Estate Agent**
- **The Multi-Million Dollar Real Estate Agent**
- **Love What You Do and Sell Houses**
- **Stop Selling Houses and Sell Yourself**
- **List It, Sell It, Go to Cabo**
- **Sell Your Soul to the Devil: Sell 100 Houses a Year**
- **Just Say "No" to Baking Cookies and Cold Calling**
- **Be The Ball and Sell Your Way to a Million Dollars**
- **Coffee is for Closers: I Sell Houses**
- **Love and The Real Estate Agent: Sell with Passion**
- **The Co-Dependent Agent: Why Can't I Move In With You?**
- **The Art of Real Estate Maintenance**
- **The 80 Hour Work Week: Real Estate is Hard Work**

What do you think? Any of these catch your eye? A little bit of fun here of course, and I bet you recognize some of the real books and movies I reference. When you write a book one of the biggest obstacles you face is coming up with a title that is interesting and captures the "spirit" of your message. I committed the cardinal sin of writing, and started writing this book without a real title for it in mind.

Then something interesting happened: I started doing research for the book with consumers. I posed the following questions to people:

- **What do you value in a real estate agent?**
- **What is important to you when choosing an agent?**
- **What do you expect from your real estate agent when buying or selling your home?**

These were three very straightforward questions for the public. The responses were very interesting and I include all of them in this book. What surprised me is that one word kept popping up over and over in each of the responses: *honesty.* Consumers want and expect their real estate agent to be honest and truthful with them and look out for their best interests instead of just being focused on making a commission on the sale.

The research I did gave me the title for the book, **The Honest Real Estate Agent.** It's not that exciting and maybe a little boring. I really like it though because it fits in exactly with what consumers want and expect from real estate agents today and into the future. I believe that this honesty carries through to the rest of your life. You need to be honest with yourself, other agents, your family, your work habits, your continuing education and your commitment to building your business. Honesty is an integral part of being successful today in any career you choose.

I know what you are probably saying, *"The Honest Real Estate Agent*? Of course I am honest, why would anyone think otherwise? Is this guy being silly or something?"* My response is that I appreciate and respect your thoughts. I expect all of you are honest since we learn about being honest from the time we are little kids and throughout our lifetime. "Don't take money from the cookie jar." "Don't cheat on your test." "Did you throw rocks at that train? Tell me the truth." This is not what I am talking about. By now we all should have a sense of what is right and wrong.

I am talking about being honest with your clients from your first meeting, through the entire sales process and all the way to the closing. Your clients are going to rely on you for your honesty, knowledge and advice from beginning to end. You as the real estate agent have to be brave and have the confidence to always be honest with your clients. You will be fighting an internal battle with yourself between making sales happen and honestly advising your clients even if it means killing a deal. Clients today want and value your honesty when they hire you to be their real estate agent.

For example, your client says to you, "Wow, this is a great house, I really like it, and it has exactly the type of floor plan we want. What do you think of this neighborhood? Is it nice?" In your mind you are already struggling on how to respond. Here are your thoughts: "Man, I really need this deal, I haven't had a closing in three months. I thought these buyers were going to be easy. What do I say? Do I tell them the truth, or do I tell them what they want to hear since they like the house so much?"

Another example: your client says, "I will not clean the garage out, it's too much work and buyers don't care about garages." How do you respond to that as a real estate agent? Are you intimidated by your seller? You have to have the confidence to push back and explain to your seller that he has to clean out the garage in order to sell the house at the price he wants. If you don't have the confidence to push back and let the issue slide then you are not being honest to your client.

You have been helping a buyer and you are visiting a house they really like for the third time and today is the day they plan on submitting an offer with you as their agent. The night before you find out from a contact you have in the City Government that the open land behind this house has just been approved for a strip mall including a gas station. What do you do? It will not be developed at least for another year. Do you tell your buyers? Or do you move forward with the offer because you need the business badly?

Being honest is doing what is right for your clients. Your clients are counting on you and they need you to be their advocate and protector. If you don't do it, then who will? The goodwill you build by always being honest with your clients is what will create long lasting customer relationships, referrals for new clients and repeat business.

In this book, I am going to be honest with you about what it takes to be a real estate agent. It is not an easy job and at times it can be a very challenging job, especially in the first few years. Some of the topics I will discuss are the following:

- Why do people hate real estate agents?
- Use the Sherlock Holmes method for helping buyers.
- You can be in your 20s and be successful in real estate.
- Twelve characteristics and traits for being a successful real estate agent.
- What do I wish I had known before I got my real estate license?
- What do people really want and value from real estate agents?
- The "Honesty Conflict" with your clients.
- Take the Time Management Quiz and see if you pass.
- What are you selling?
- What does the future real estate agent look like?
- Use the Napoleon Hill method for finding mentors.
- What is your niche going to be?
- Be yourself and have fun in your career.
- I did it "My Way" like Frank Sinatra.

I will tell you my story about how I became a real estate agent and in the Appendix I will share stories from other agents about how they got into real estate as a career.

Our life is all about choices, and I will provide you with the information and inspiration so you can choose to be a successful real estate agent for many years to come. I have written this book for you so you can be happy and productive in your new career.

Chapter 1
An Unexpected Life

"We must let go the life we have planned, so as to accept the one that is waiting for us." This is a quote from Joseph Campbell, American Philosopher and Mythologist of the 20th Century. When we are graduating from college we all have in our mind a road map of where we want our lives to go. I am going to get this type of job, get this advanced degree, marry by 30, have kids by the time I am 35. But, most times we don't end up living the life we had planned.

Has your life gone exactly the way you had thought it would? Mine has not. You can say the same for most real estate agents. This is a career most people get into after they have had at least one or two jobs after college or high school. Have you ever heard a college student say: "I want to be a real estate agent; it has been my lifelong dream." I don't think so.

I wrote this book for those of you who might be considering a career change. I am here to tell you that being a real estate agent is an excellent choice as a career path. Before we jump into this book together I want you to do a little exercise. Get a piece of paper or open up a Word document on your computer. Write down this question: "What are the characteristics of my ideal job?" Stop reading and complete this exercise right now. Try to come up with at least three to four points describing your ideal job.

Here's a list I came up with that most people would agree with:

- Doing work that is meaningful where my product or service makes a difference in the lives of my customers.
- A job which is secure, so I don't have to constantly be worrying about being laid off.
- Challenging work—I don't want to be bored with my job.
- Not much travel—I don't want to have to be on the road a lot and away from my family.
- A job that I enjoy doing and gives me satisfaction daily.
- Make good money, but more importantly I want to be building something for myself towards the future with my business.

Did any of these items pop up on your list? This list describes the job and career of a real estate agent. It is a meaningful service that you provide to your clients by helping them buy or sell their home, and it is a commission-paying job. The nature of a commission-paying job is that you have little to no security, but when you do a good job you are rewarded. Once you have established yourself as a real estate agent it is a secure job. To establish yourself can take anywhere from one to two years, but the time is worthwhile because it does pay off in the long run.

With a lot of jobs being outsourced, a real estate agent is a "belly to belly" sales job which can't be moved overseas. The work is challenging because you are working with different types of people in various situations. You are compensated for the value and skills you bring to the marketplace, so if you are good at what you do you will make a good income. Traveling is generally not a part of being a real estate agent since your territory is usually close to where you live. It is a fun job and you do get daily satisfaction in spite of all the challenges you face.

You can make as much money as you want based on how many hours you put in. You have to look at yourself as an entrepreneur, and the business you build over time will become easier with repeat clients and referrals from past clients. I will go into more detail on each of these points, but I want to state up front that a career in real estate is a very fulfilling and profitable career choice.

How many real estate agents do you know? How many real estate agents are there in your city? How many real estate agents are there in the world? You can probably say "a lot" in response to each of these questions. Seems like everywhere you turn you run into a real estate agent.

I bet you are thinking the following:

- "As a new agent how can I compete against so many experienced real estate agents?"
- "Where do I start? I know a lot of people who have gone into real estate only to change jobs after a year or two and leave the industry completely."
- "At this point in my life I can't afford to make any mistakes. I think I can be a good real estate agent, but do I have what it takes to be successful?"

My objective in this book is to help you become a successful real estate agent as you start your new career. I am going to share with you some marketing strategies you can implement right away at little or no cost to you. I make you this promise up front that I will not suggest or ask you to do any of the following: prospect and cold call people on the telephone, door to door canvassing, bake cookies, hand-write and mail 200 cards to people you know on a monthly basis, send refrigerator magnets with your picture on them, mail sports schedules, or do any type of print advertising in a newspaper or magazine.

In addition, I will not request you attend a high priced sales seminar, buy a costly coaching program, buy a contact management software program, buy a lead generation product, or any type of sales selling system. All of these methods are time consuming, costly and they represent the past. You need to set yourself apart from your competition and build an identity and brand for yourself moving forward.

The new paradigm for successful real estate agents is marketing and promoting yourself as the product rather than begging (I mean selling) people to work with you. Today's customers are more informed and educated on real estate so they will choose a real estate agent who will offer them the expertise and value they demand and require. The touchy feely marketing methods of the past with cookies, calendars, refrigerator magnets, apple butter at the door, and sports schedules are not what customers want today. They want to have a professional expert in their area of need represent and advise them.

By following what I present in this book you will discover that clients will come to you, rather than you having to find them. When you build your expertise and value, clients will find you and ask you to be their real estate agent.

I will give you the strategies and methods necessary to be successful today and into the future. There has never been a better time to start a career as a real estate agent. The Baby Boomer generation is getting older, which means in the next five to ten years there will be a lot of real estate agents retiring from the business. The opportunity is ideal for anyone who is ready to take on the challenge.

Don't be wary of how the real estate market is, because even during slow times there are real estate agents who do quite well and make a good living helping their clients buy and sell their homes. If you are a top-skilled and valuable real estate agent you will always be in demand and you will continue to make a good income regardless of market conditions.

In the new economy, being a real estate agent is a secure and profitable job option. Once you have built your brand and your business as an agent you'll find that you have flexibility, security and an income that a lot of other jobs do not offer.

Chapter 2
Is It Time to Change?

What is a good training ground for being successful in real estate? This is a tough question because there are so many real estate agents who had different work and life experiences before they got into real estate. For example, I know successful agents who came from a variety of fields such as: School Teacher, Corporate Sales, Human Resources, Stay-at-Home Mom or Dad, Lawyer, Retail Sales, and Property Management.

Here is my brief story about how and why I became a real estate agent. For years after graduating from college I was a sales representative, account manager and sales manager in the world of high tech software sales. In 1999, I had my best year ever from an earnings standpoint. I managed a geographic region and our team blew it out; we were the number one sales division in our company. That year I W2'd over $200,000. It was awesome. We celebrated and had a blast at the year-end company sales convention and I never felt so good about myself in my sales career than I did at that moment.

Then the next year started and everything fell apart. Our quotas increased exponentially, we lost a good portion of our territory and then I started losing key members of the sales team. I had to start all over again and I had built no equity at all in myself or with my company in the product I was selling. It was the worst I ever felt in my career. This was my moment of epiphany. I had always gone through the ups and downs each year with higher quotas and new compensation plans, but this year was the most difficult. I felt since we had done so well the year before that the next year would be a little easier. Well, that's not how it works in the world of corporate sales. So my epiphany right then and there was that I had to change jobs and get into something where I could build equity in myself based on my past sales.

In 2000, my job odyssey started. I worked for four companies that year and I received four W2's at the end of the year. It was an amazing follow up to my great year in 1999. I finally ended up working in a sales and management position selling corporate housing to companies and individuals who needed temporary housing. This was an excellent transition job for me to get into real estate because I learned a lot about the relocation industry.

I decided to become a real estate agent because I felt I had good qualifications in order to be successful in the field. First, I was an excellent salesperson, had professional experience in corporate sales, and had gone through numerous sales training courses and seminars over the years. I had lived in the area where I would be a real estate agent for most of my life so I knew the cities, towns, schools and neighborhoods extremely well. I had a lot of contacts through my family, friends, and prior work associates, which gave me a good contact list to cultivate. Lastly, I felt the biggest thing I had going for me is that everyone needs a house to live in, so the amount of potential customers was infinite in comparison to the defined territories of my corporate sales jobs.

In 2002, I attended a real estate school, took and passed the state exam and then got my real estate license. In 2003, I joined RE/MAX and I was completely on my own. I was recently married with a baby on the way and I was starting a new career. I have to be honest and admit it was a very scary and stressful time for me to make such a big career change. Now looking back I can't believe I did it and I am so thankful and grateful that I did make the switch.

I have built a good business for myself and it did take a few years. I make a good living and I am my own boss. I can work as many hours as I want in a week based on how many clients I am helping. If I want to work 80 hours a week, I can choose to do so. If I want to cut back and only work 30 hours one week, I can choose to do so. I enjoy my job immensely. Having a flexible job allows me to spend more time with my family.

I am receiving repeat business from past clients, and getting referrals from my past clients and my sphere of contacts. I am also generating new business as a result of what I have built for myself with my reputation, my web page and my online resources. It is the best job I have ever had in my life. I feel really good about myself and what I do for a living, because I make a big difference in the lives of my clients when I help them buy or sell their home. On a personal level it's fulfilling because I am in charge of my business and who I am as a person.

One of the myths of being a real estate agent is that you have to be "older" to be successful. This is not true at all. **You can be young and successful in real estate.** I think this has changed a lot in the past ten years with more and more people in their 20s becoming real estate agents.

Prior to getting into real estate, I was in high-tech in my late 30s and was considered "old" in my field. One of the last companies I worked for before I got into real estate had a CEO who was younger than me. It was a good-sized company that had recently gone public on NASDAQ and the CEO was already a multi-millionaire. My manager was also younger than me. It was the first time in my life that I had a manager who was younger than me. It was kind of weird, but he was a good guy and I did learn a lot from him. We are still in touch today.

Then I went into real estate and joined RE/MAX Alliance in Louisville, Colorado, which is ten minutes away from Boulder, Colorado. I was 41 years old when I started at RE/MAX with 40 other agents in the office and I was the third youngest agent in the office. At that time there were two other guys who were in their 30s and everyone else was older than me. I felt great and so young again. It was such a rush for me when I started out at RE/MAX.

I have only lost one potential client over the years because the prospective client wanted someone with more experience than I had. At the time, I had six years experience and the prospective client wanted someone with 20+ years experience. I never felt I was not qualified or incapable in my first five years of being an agent and servicing my clients. I felt this way because I believed in myself and knew I had the skills and expertise to help my clients.

Today, it's more common to see real estate agents who are in their 20s and a lot of them are doing quite well. I am so excited to see new and younger people joining our profession. This is the best way for all of us as real estate agents to make sure we have a viable and secure career in the future. Our profession needs to attract the best and brightest who want to be in the business and I welcome all of you. I don't look at you as competition because we are all in this together. The more professional agents I have on the other side of transactions, the easier it is for me to be successful on my end. Most times we need a professional and qualified real estate agent on each end of the deal to ensure a successful closing.

My advice to those of you in your 20s is to not be intimidated by the "old guard" in our field. Jump in with enthusiasm and vigor because it is a great long-term career. If I had been ready and qualified to be a real estate agent in my 20s I would have been able to build a more solid and secure business as I have gotten older. I urge you to continue reading because I want to share with you how being a real estate agent can be an excellent career choice for you.

Chapter 3
What I Wish I'd Known Before Getting My License

Becoming a real estate agent is very easy when you compare it to other careers. Can you imagine someone becoming a doctor in under three months? The entire process for becoming a medical doctor can take up to ten years after graduating from college. How about a lawyer? You need to go to law school for three years after college and then pass the state bar exam where you want to practice. How about a CPA? A dentist? I think you get my point. In contrast, almost anyone can get a real estate license. It's pretty simple. All you need to do is go to a real estate school in your area, then take and pass your state exam, and you will receive your real estate license.

It is pretty straightforward to get licensed as a real estate agent, but the real test is taking that license and making an income that you can live off of by building your own business. I tell people I know that being a real estate agent is one of the easiest jobs to get into, but the hardest to stay in over time.

Here are some things you need to know before getting your license:

1) **"The Snowball Effect": As a real estate agent, you will not have a steady paycheck.** Your income is not going to be a steady paycheck twice a month like most jobs. The commissions you will receive come only when you close a transaction and there is no set timetable on this. You can go months without having a closing and then in one month you can have three closings. The roller coaster effect with your income is easily the biggest challenge you will face in real estate. A lot of new real estate agents cannot handle this and leave the industry within a year. A good rule of thumb is that it can take up to one to two years before you build a profitable business model as an agent.

How do you offset this? Ideally, it would be nice to have an amount of money set aside prior to starting your career in real estate and be able to tap into it during the slow months. Depending on the company you work for, it might be possible to create a pay structure that will help you through the early times when you have slow periods. What is key is keeping your costs as low as possible. Don't get in over your head with a lot of marketing campaigns in your first year. I will describe to you a first year marketing campaign that costs less than $1,000 later in this book. A lot of new agents have grandiose ideas about building a huge business in their first year. Usually this is not realistic. Think of a snowball. Start building it slowly from the ground up and over time it will get bigger and bigger.

2) No Man Is an Island: you'll face ruthless competition as a real estate agent. It's all up to you because it is a very competitive business. The other real estate agents in your office generally do not care if you are successful or not. They view you as competition for their business. You have to be the type of person who can get things done on your own and not be intimidated by other agents in your office and area where you work. This also depends upon the office and real estate agent business model you are working within. I will discuss this more in Chapter 11.

3) You'll be your own boss. Can you manage yourself? Being your own boss is what a lot of people want but then they realize they can't manage themselves. You have to have the discipline, willpower and strength to do the right thing every day for the success of your business. Again, this is why a lot of new agents fail. They do not stay focused on doing the work every day. "Do I really need to write my blog today and go to that networking meeting? I think I'll go play golf instead since it's such a beautiful day and I can easily get a tee time since everyone else is working." The small decisions you make daily as your own boss will determine your success. If you blow work off and procrastinate it will catch up with you at the end of the year and you will fail.

4) Can you sell? Are you a good negotiator? As a real estate agent, you must master the art of persuasion. It's one thing to enjoy decorating houses to get them ready to sell like you might see on some of the reality TV shows. This is a very small part of what you do as a real estate agent. You are constantly negotiating one thing or the other with many different people, not just your clients. You have to negotiate with other real estate agents, title representatives, mortgage lenders, and other service related people. The way you are compensated is based on how well you negotiate with your clients as well.

There will be many hurdles you have to overcome during the sales process and you have to sell through them to make it to a successful closing. You need to have a strong personality so you can lead your clients through the sales process. It would be ideal if you have some type of sales experience and I do realize a lot of people have innate sales skills without even knowing it. What's important is to understand the psychology and mechanics of selling. There are a lot of excellent books out there that can help you. Here are a few I highly recommend:

The One Minute Salesperson by Spencer Johnson and Larry Wilson
SPIN Selling by Neil Rackham
The New Conceptual Selling (2005) Robert B. Miller and Stephen E. Heiman

If you read these three books you will have a good foundation for basic sales skills, with one caveat: you have to read them! I read so many sales books and listened to a lot of audio tapes on selling in my early years and it did pay off for me. I am always amazed when I hear that so many people do not read nor study for their career. Since you are reading this book right now, I know you are different. You have already taken the initiative. Read these three books and you will not be disappointed. Be different, invest the time, and continue to build your skills and knowledge.

To improve your negotiating skills I highly recommend you attain the following designation: **Certified Negotiation Expert (CNE)**. I attended this two-day class recently and it was by far one of the best continuing education classes I have attended. Contact your local Realtor Association to find out the next time this class will be taught in your area. This class is money well spent for improving your negotiating skills.

5) **Patience is a virtue.** How patient are you? You can't be successful as a real estate agent unless you have the utmost patience in helping your clients and working with other agents on transactions. Some buyers take a long time to make a buying decision and you have to be there, working hard with them until they are ready. You might have to go through three to four contracts on a single transaction before the deal sticks and you make it to the closing. Some buyers can take up to a year until they reach a closing. And the same is true for sellers. You can have a listing active for a year until you get it under contract and make it to a successful closing. Not all sales situations will take this long but it's something for you to be aware of to make sure you have the patience.

6) **Do you get bogged down in details?** There is a tremendous amount of paperwork and details in executing contracts for your clients. Do you like paperwork and contracts? The good thing nowadays is that most of this is automated and the process is a lot easier than when I started out years ago. In order to be successful, however, a real estate agent needs to be accurate and detail-oriented for his or her clients.

It will make things a lot easier if you are okay with the items on this list. There are a lot of other factors to being successful as a real estate agent, but if you don't feel comfortable with these six items then you might want to reconsider going into real estate. For example, you can be a great salesperson and very persuasive but if you are deficient in details and managing your time then you will not succeed.

Chapter 4
Do You Have What It Takes?

At some point during this process you probably have asked yourself: do I have the ability to be a successful real estate agent? This is a great question because it would be really helpful to find out before getting your real estate license. There will be a substantial investment of your time and money in starting a career in real estate so it is helpful to get an idea if it's a good fit for you.

Here is my list of **twelve characteristics and traits** that will define you as a successful real estate agent today and into the future:

1) **You are a people person**. Most important and top of my list is the ability and desire to build relationships with clients. Buying or selling a home is the biggest financial transaction most people make in their lives. It is very important to the client that they have a real estate agent they value, trust, and respect. The best real estate agents create lasting relationships with their clients so they have a customer for life, which leads to repeat business and referrals. Your clients want to know that you care about them as people and you are not motivated only by making a commission. Buying or selling a home is stressful and complex for most people so they really need to have a real estate agent who is on their side and helping them through the process.

2) **You are an optimist.** You need to be strong to ride out the dry months when you don't have any closings. You have to realize that Spring is going to come after Winter. The deals will happen but the slow months can definitely take a toll on your psyche. Having a high level of self esteem can be an asset here, since it gives you the confidence to ride out the difficult times. Believe me all real estate agents face slow times during the year and during their career.

3) **You deal with rejection and/or failure well.** To be successful in sales you have to have a short memory. When you lose a buyer or a listing, you can't dwell on it. Learn from it, figure out what you would do differently the next time and then move on. The good thing about real estate is that there are plenty of fish in the sea. You will get another customer. I know a lot of salespeople who are devastated when they lose a customer or a deal and it puts them into a funk and then they don't do anything for days. They just wallow in their despair and lose all self confidence. You

have to have the ability to not let rejection or lost sales bother you and do not take it personally.

One prediction I can make with absolute certainty to you is that in your career as a real estate agent you will lose a buyer, you will lose a listing, you will have a contract fall apart and you will lose a sale. You cannot sell to everyone and get every contract to a closing. It just doesn't happen every time. The sooner you accept and realize this fact the more productive and happier you will be in your career.

4) **You have the maturity and ability to handle difficult, delicate or emotional situations.** As a real estate agent you will confront personal situations with your clients that are stressful such as the following:

- You will have couples who openly fight in front of you when they are either buying or selling a home.

- You will help a couple buy a home and then in the future they will contact you and tell you they are getting divorced and need to sell their home. Divorce situations can be hard on you, especially if you know the clients well.

- Estate sales can also be emotional when you are dealing with the death of someone you might have known and then working with the family and executor of the will.

- You will help clients at one point who are downsizing from their family home and moving to a smaller place. It's not unusual to be at this type of closing and to have the seller or sellers crying because they have to sell their home.

- Short sales and foreclosures are also very difficult and hard on your clients.

- You have to have the emotional strength to be strong and not let these situations take a toll on you personally.

5) **You are a good multi-tasker**. Are you a good juggler? As a real estate agent you need to be able to work on multiple tasks at the same time and jump from one task to another with ease. What's difficult is when you go from an intense situation on the phone and then have to jump to a completely different type of call. I have had times when I have been negotiating details of a deal with another agent. When my client calls me and I'm in the middle of a call such as this, I have to tamp down my intensity and energy so I don't blow them away.

There are also times when you are out showing properties and then you have an important call come in on your cell phone that you have to take. It's not an ideal situation to have to talk on the phone while you're out showing a house. Other times you can be working on a very detailed contract on your computer and one of your office staff comes to your desk asking for help with something. Most jobs nowadays you have to juggle tasks, but what is hard as a real estate agent is managing your emotions in the process. You don't want to vent or lose your temper with your clients or with another agent. Maintaining a level of professionalism and calm will help you be more successful and enjoy your job more.

6) **You are a winner.** Does it bother you when you lose? This is very obvious and of course no one likes to lose. This is critical to real estate agents because you are competing all the time. You are competing with other agents for clients, competing with other agents on properties if you are representing a buyer, competing with other houses for sale when you have a listing and you're competing with yourself to make sure you attain your goals. And in real estate you will lose. Accept it, because you are not going to get every potential client you meet. What is important is what you do about it when you lose a client or deal. Are you going to pout? Are you going to hide in your office and not make any more calls? You have to have a winning attitude and get back to work and focus on getting the next client or deal. Controlling your negative emotions after something bad happens is what will set you apart from your competition. No whining or complaining is allowed in real estate.

7) **You are responsible.** Since you are your own boss you have to be responsible for yourself and your business. Being responsible requires discipline and focus to make sure you do the daily activities and work each day. It's very easy to slack off and procrastinate when you work for yourself. You need to have goals which challenge and stretch you to be the best you can be. Don't go easy on yourself. If you have a spouse or significant other then this will be easier for you. Almost every day after work my wife asks me, "anything new today?" This helps me stay focused and on track because I don't want to make "the Boss" at home angry.

8) **You're like Spock, not like Kirk.** *Star Trek* fans, you can relate to this. Spock is the calm, unemotional thinker and Kirk is the embodiment of going with your gut and letting your feelings guide you. I am not saying to be a robot. Rather, make sure you don't let your emotions get in the way of doing your job. I have been in many situations where I have seen other real estate agents lose their cool and act unprofessionally. Remember when you are helping your clients you have to always maintain your composure. You never vent, complain or get angry around your clients. Never!

9) **You are creative.** This is important today and especially going into the future. The successful real estate agents are the ones who are always thinking about their

job and how they can improve and generate more business. We have all heard of "working smarter, not harder." One of the most rewarding things about real estate is creating and trying new processes and methods. This is especially fun and exciting when you hit on something that works—and you thought of it!

10) **You have physical stamina.** There is a lot of physical work involved with helping clients. I've had days where I have shown over 20 houses to buyers. On days such as these when I go to bed at night my legs are burning. During the year you can have stretches where you work every day without a day off. I remember one summer where I literally worked every day straight from July 5th until the Labor Day Weekend without a break. It's great to be busy and do well, but you need to have the physical stamina to keep up. Maintain a good exercise schedule year round to stay fit so your body can handle the really busy times you do have.

11) **You pay attention to details.** Being detail-oriented is especially important when it comes to contracts and paperwork for your clients. You have to be fully committed to making sure all of the contracts you execute for your clients are accurate. You can't coast on this one because your clients are counting on you to get it right for them.

12) **You have enthusiasm for life.** You do need a high level of enthusiasm so people who work with you feel confident in you as a person and enjoy spending time with you. I am not talking about being cheesy and over the top happy all the time. You need to feel good about yourself and enjoy being a real estate agent because your clients will pick this up and it will make them feel better about you.

What do you think after reading this list? Do you have what it takes? Are you up for the challenge? I think you are, otherwise you would be not be reading this book. Don't worry if you don't have all of these qualities yet; many of them can be nurtured and developed over time.

Chapter 5
I Hate Real Estate Agents

Have you told any of your friends or family that you plan on being a real estate agent? What type of responses do you get? Probably kind of lukewarm. "Really? You want to be a real estate agent? Why is that?" I think the public perception of real estate as a career might be at an all time low. The decade of the 2000s was not a good one for real estate around the country and the public feels that a number of real estate agents contributed to the problems in some capacity. Unfortunately, when you have so many people working in a profession you are going to have some who are dishonest, unscrupulous and downright criminal. I could recount many horror stories where an unsuspecting person bought a house at an inflated price. A year or two later they could not sell the house, and it either became a "short-sale" or a "foreclosure."

I have read stories about builders, real estate agents, lenders, and appraisers who conspired together to sell artificially inflated properties in a new subdivision. The new owners of these homes ended up owing more money on their mortgages than what they could sell the house for on the open market. This practice is illegal, and the resulting foreclosures decimated the subdivision. Unlawful activities like these contributed to the foreclosure crisis in the late 2000s.

For years the jokes used to be about how bad lawyers can be, but lately real estate agents have almost as bad a reputation. The bad feelings towards real estate agents are real and you need to be aware of what you are getting yourself into as you start your career.

My strategy for countering bad feelings about real estate agents is to first understand why a lot of people hate us. As real estate agents I believe we need to confront these perceptions head-on in order to do something about them. I have compiled actual comments I have heard over the years from friends, colleagues and family. Here are some of the reasons people say they hate real estate agents:

1) They are dishonest.

2) They only care about closing the deal and making a sale. They do not care about the buyer or seller as long as they get their commission.

3) They are lazy. They will only do the minimal amount of work required to receive their commission. They are usually playing golf when you need them.

4) Some of them are cocky and arrogant, don't treat people well and they are very pushy.

5) They don't share all of the information about a house or its history to potential buyers.

6) I can never get them on the phone, it always goes to voice mail and then it takes forever for them to call me back.

7) They don't listen. I asked my agent to show me houses in a specific price range and then I was shown a bunch of houses above my price target. Very frustrating!

8) They make a lot of money for hardly working at all. I mean, how hard can it be?

My advice is to accept the fact that people feel this way and then do your best to show them that you are the complete opposite of everything on the list. It will make your job easier to develop and follow a business model based on what people really want from real estate agents. What would that list look like? Here is what I have heard from people over the years:

1) I want a real estate agent who is honest and trustworthy and who is always looking out for my best interest. I want them to negotiate the best deal possible for me.

2) If there are problems with a house I am buying, I want to know. For example, if someone has committed suicide in the house and my agent knows, then I expect them to tell me.

3) I want an agent who is a hard worker, who works full time and is committed to their job.

4) I want an agent who is experienced and knowledgeable in what I need and want.

5) I want an agent who will answer the phone when I call and who is a good communicator via email and texts.

6) I want an agent who listens to me and does what I ask them to do.

7) I want an agent who enjoys their job and makes our real estate experience more enjoyable and not so serious.

This is a very reasonable list. This is exactly what I would expect to receive from a real estate agent if I hired one. If you focus on the basics and just take care of your clients, your business will succeed and grow over time.

Here's a secret: even someone with very negative feelings about real estate agents can become a believer! Some of my best clients over the years have been the ones who had a bad experience with a real estate agent in the past. When they found me and I made them happy with my level of service and professionalism, we built rapport. The resulting relationship was much stronger because I exceeded their expectations and they were very thankful and grateful they worked with me.

Finally, there is a business model out there that you may be pressured to use that can do serious damage to your career and reputation. It can lead people to dislike and even hate you as a real estate agent. Some real estate companies promote the "friends and family plan" with their new agents. If you are familiar with sales, this is simply a variation on the "churn and burn" model. These companies hire new agents with the intention of squeezing out as many deals as they can from the new agent's friends and family. Beware of this scenario! The company is taking the easy way out. Instead of providing the resources needed to succeed, they "use" their new agents for their network of friends and family. This inevitably yields a handful of deals from new agents before they quit. If you find yourself in this situation, you'll be pressured to "hard sell" all of your relatives and friends. When this fails to help you build a successful business, you'll not only have to leave your career in real estate, you'll do damage to your most valuable relationships as well. As salespeople, there are few things as vital to our success as our relationships and reputations.

Chapter 6
What Do Clients Want and Expect from You?

For more information about what clients really want from us, let's go to the source. I posed the following questions to a number of people I know to find out what the public wants from real estate agents. None of the people who provided me their comments were my clients either currently or in the past; I wanted people who would speak freely about this issue.

- **What do you value in a real estate agent?**
- **What is important to you in choosing an agent?**
- **What do you expect from your real estate agent? (when buying or selling your home)**

Here are some of the responses: (I have included additional responses in Appendix B)

Cammy from Denver: "Online tools have made finding a property so much easier for a buyer but they haven't replaced the expertise needed during the negotiation and contract process. When I've bought or sold homes, I've expected my real estate agent to know the legal ins-and-outs of a contract and have attention to detail. I also expect my agent to know the neighborhood and have great contacts with other local agents. Lastly, and most importantly, I hire a real estate agent to honestly advise me. A very successful local area real estate agent assisted us in buying a house about 12 years ago that was absolutely a horrible investment in an unsavory neighborhood. The agent never uttered a word of caution and my husband and I think we must have been experiencing temporary insanity when we bought that place."

Jeff from San Francisco, Investor: "Education, my real estate agents have provided a ton of education on their theory for making money in the market. It's definitely worked out for me in the long run. My agents are always available even if it's a stupid question, or if it is advice years after our last transaction. Build a partnering relationship between the two of you. A joint mission based on explicit criteria.

I don't want to be bothered with stuff that doesn't meet criteria, and I don't want to go on open houses every Sunday. That's what real estate agents do, they find the properties for their clients. And I especially don't want to see criteria changing, in order to make a sale.

Have a network of trusted auxiliary professionals for reference to your client. And be honest about their capabilities. This all adds up to they are not just some wheeler-dealers trying to get me to buy something. They are active partners in my real estate investment strategy."

Po from Dallas: "It goes without saying that I expect honesty from my real estate agent. That and their expertise in the local market. When it comes to selling, I want them to tell me what I need to do in order to maximize my asking price (painting walls, flower beds, de-cluttering, etc.) I also want them to make sure that they price it according to what objectives I have. For instance, if I want to sell quickly, what price do I need to be? If I'm looking for the highest price and don't have to sell immediately, let me know that price. Give me options. I want to know that I'm getting value for the commission I am paying out.

When we bought our home, we used a friend of my in-laws. He was a well established real estate agent and very helpful. He knew how to negotiate down the price. We saved $50K off of the list price. Since he is a friend of the family and saved us a lot of money, we'll end up using him when we sell and buy another home. He always sends us calendars and comes over and sees the kids. The relationship is key, but he also provided us with value in the knowledge he provides. He even pulls comps for us when it comes time to dispute the property tax assessment."

Carlos from New Jersey: "I really look for a real estate agent to be familiar with the neighborhoods I am looking at. What are the schools like? Mostly young couples? Families? And overall, just a general sense that the agent is listening to you and really trying to match you up with what you are looking for and is not just motivated by the 'sale.' "

Sima from Utah: "I value and appreciate a real estate agent who will show me homes in the price range that I want and specified and not what the agent thinks I should do. And I don't want to work with an agent who takes things so seriously. A sense of humor is what we appreciate the most."

Marc from Maryland: "What I look for in a real estate agent is really no different than what I look for in a sales person of any type. This person should know their product. In this case the local neighborhoods, school systems, house inventory and such. The real estate agent should be well versed in the selling process and be prepared to overcome any challenges that come up. The agent should listen to what my needs are and present product that fulfills those needs. I don't have time to go see a 3 bedroom house that is old and is in need of repair when I said I wanted a 4 bedroom house that would be "turnkey." I want an agent that is well connected within their community so that they have access to the resources available to expedite the sale. And a successful track record is a requirement as well."

Bob from Denver: "I would say give some general information when we meet for the first time, be a good negotiator, be honest, share the information with the client.

When I am buying: understand what I am looking for, refine the search criteria based on my budget and my needs, and be honest. I didn't like the first agent I started working with, because she was just using her computer to do a computer-search on Multiple Listing Service (MLS) and I could do that myself.

When I am selling: present the property the best they can, and give me solid information on how much the property really is worth. No marketing crap!"

Greg from Maryland: "Honesty! I worked with a real estate agent who during a conversation regarding a house I liked kept saying: 'But it has NO basement.' He thought buying a single story home with no basement in this city was a bad move and would be in far less demand when it came time to sell it. This directly addressed a concern I had when we first met, to buy a home that would be easy to sell.

He knew a lot about real estate and based our conversations on things that were important to me. Most real estate agents spend too much time trying to convince you it is a good time to buy. He however told me an equal number of horror and success stories, and backed them up with facts. I remember one time we were talking about renovating homes. He then showed me two homes on the market that had been renovated, one where the owners were priced to lose money and one where the owners were likely to make a good profit. During the conversation I learned quite a bit, including the importance of a house's footprint. I also realized there was quite a bit about real estate I would likely never know and was glad I had an expert opinion I could rely on."

Ann from Virginia: "What do I value in a real estate agent? Well, first honesty. I'd likely choose an agent based on reputation. I expect an agent to keep me informed of all things related to sale of the property—both good and bad."

Karrie from Seattle: "I look for two main things in my real estate agent. The first is what I call 'subject matter expertise.' The process is daunting and there are a lot of ways you can be taken advantage of. I want to know that my agent has my best interests in mind, both long and short term, and isn't afraid to stand up to me or others in the process to state it. They should be able to help me understand the entire process so I'm an active participant in every step. I don't want to sit on the side-lines while everything is happening. I want to be educated about the process so I can be knowledgeable about the whole thing. It's frustrating that the process is so confusing, even to an educated home-buyer, so I want an agent who will take the time to help me understand.

Second, I want my real estate agent to understand my priorities. They should have an understanding of what it is I'm looking for in a home. That sounds obvious, but after spending some time with us, my agent had an idea of what we were looking for and would actually point out flaws in a home that would be potential problems, things that I might have over-looked but that she noticed. She also was forthcoming in what things were easy to change and what things weren't worth compromising on."

Jeanine from Maryland: "In a real estate agent I value trust, knowledge, and the ability to listen. Buying a home is a big decision and not one that us young people make lightly. I must feel like I can trust that the agent is working in my best interest. I need to know that they understand what I am looking for and that they will not stray outside the guidelines that I have set. In order for them to do this they must be a great listener. They also need to be very knowledgeable in terms of what the current market is like, how to work contracts, and what a fair price is. If I trust my agent, they listen to what I want and more importantly what I don't want, and they know real estate inside and out they will have my business.

I expect my real estate agent to work hard, work consistently, and be timely. Those three things will allow them to not miss out on any potential opportunities. I also expect my real estate agent to have great negotiation skills when dealing with other agents. I wouldn't want to miss an opportunity because my agent was not at the top of their game."

One of the best ways to learn as a salesperson is to find out what your customers really want and expect from you. What do you think of these comments? Can you live up to the expectations of these clients? I will review their comments in more detail in the next chapter.

Chapter 7
Honesty, Expertise and an Agent Who Has My Back

The comments in the previous chapter by people about what they want and expect from real estate agents and what they value are very instructive. Here are some conclusions you can take away from the comments, especially when looking to the future trends in our industry.

Honesty. Did you notice how many times where "honest" and "honesty" are stated? This blew me away because so many people want the same thing. Our clients want us to be truthful with them whenever they have a question or an issue that comes up which requires an explanation from us. People want to know that we are looking out for their best interests and being honest. This includes being forthcoming about what we know, even if it means that this specific deal could fall apart because of what we say. What people don't want is a real estate agent who is protecting a deal at their expense. They want to know the truth about potential problems or issues. They realize that even if it's not what they want to hear at the moment, the truth will help them in the long run. Clients want so badly to have a real estate agent who is **HONEST** with them from beginning to end. Go back and reread the comments from the people in Chapter 6 and see how many times you see "honest", "honesty", "trust", and "truthful". I have included more comments from real people just like you and me in Appendix B. Combined, the words "honest", "honesty", "trust", and "truthful" appear 24 times in Chapter 6 and Appendix B.

You're probably thinking now, "of course I am honest, this will be easy." Believe me, it's not. This is one of the biggest internal struggles you will face daily as a real estate agent when you are helping your clients. In the introduction of this book, I told you that you need to close deals and make commission in order to survive. I also mentioned that telling your clients the truth even if it means jeopardizing your commission is also part of your job as a real estate agent. You may find yourself rationalizing in your mind that you are not really lying to your client when you don't point out a problem or issue because you think it's not really that important. You want to make sure your client stays on track towards the closing so you can get your commission check. This is a slippery slope.

I have found the best way is to always tell my clients the truth about issues and potential problems when we are working together. My clients really appreciate it and they trust me, because they know I am always going to be honest with them even if it's not what they want to hear. I can justify losing some deals on the front end, and look at it this way: after we make it to the closing, I inevitably have a client for life. My clients are grateful and happy with my honesty and level of service. In turn, they are enthusiastic about referring me to their friends, colleagues and family. Don't fool yourself: this is what you need in order to survive in the long-term, rather than a quick commission based on less than the full truth. Looking out for only yourself and getting the deal on the front end really can cost you in terms of your reputation, repeat business and referrals.

Let me give you an example so you can understand this better. Let's say you are helping a buyer from out of state who is unfamiliar with the area you are showing them. They have asked you to take them back to a house they liked for a second time. The house is located in a neighborhood that you know has a lot of problems with concrete heaving. This includes shifting and cracking of driveways, sidewalks, and even home and garage foundations. Your clients ask you during the second showing about some of the cracks and heaving in the house and driveway that are clearly visible. You respond that it's not a big deal, and say that a lot of other houses in the neighborhood have similar problems. You don't discuss it anymore, even though you know it is a big deal, and a number of other houses in the neighborhood have been on the market for a long time and have gone to foreclosure because of the concrete shifting issues.

Even during the inspection phase you reassure your clients that the concrete problems are not a big deal. They move forward past the inspection based on your advice, and you make it to the closing with them. You feel a sense of relief after all is said and done, because you were able to get your clients to buy the house and you pick up a really nice commission check.

A couple of years later you run into this client at the grocery store and they are somewhat cool towards you. When you get back to the office you send them an email to check their temperature. This is the email you get back:

Hi (Insert Your Name Here),

Thanks for your email and nice seeing you today. My wife and I have been having a lot of problems recently with our house. We just had to replace our entire driveway because the concrete was cracking and shifting so much that it was dangerous for our kids to play on it. I wish you had done a better job of explaining this issue to us. Since you are local, I am sure you knew about it. My wife is pregnant and we are in process of looking to sell our house.

We had another agent stop by to talk to us. She told us it's going to be a challenge to sell the house. She was very honest with us about what we need to do in order to get the house ready to sell, which involves fixing the concrete walkways around our home and our garage foundation. This will involve a lot of expense to us. We are going to hire her as our real estate agent to sell this house and to help us buy a new one.

Sincerely,

Steve

How did you feel as you read this email from a client you were hoping to build a relationship with? If this were a real life scenario, I would bet you felt like someone just kicked you in the gut. You would realize you have just lost a ton of money, since this client will now be using a new real estate agent to both sell the house and buy a new one. You would curse and hold your head in your hands and wonder, "is this really happening?"

Yes, it is! You did not give this client honest advice and counsel when you helped them buy the house. It's not something that can just be swept under the rug, since all of the concrete problems on this house and in the neighborhood came to light quickly. Your clients remember clearly what you said and they are very upset and disappointed in you. They have chosen not to do business with you again: the ultimate rejection for a real estate agent.

What did you gain by acting this way? Perhaps one commission check, but you lost so much more in the long run. You could have made two more commission checks: one when they sold their house and another when helping them buy their next house. (Insert cussing and curse words here!) And in writing this, I made a dramatic leap by having your past client actually write you an email explaining the situation. More realistically, one day you would have noticed your past client's house listed on the market with another agent. You would never have gotten an explanation, but your now-ex-client's actions would have been crystal clear to you. You screwed up! Of course this will not happen to you because you are reading this book and will treat your clients differently than in this example.

This is just one example of how important honesty is to your reputation. Please keep this story in mind and take its message to heart. You will certainly be presented with ethical dilemmas just like this one in your career as a real estate agent. The way you choose to proceed with each client will have a ripple effect on your business. It will impact your ability to do repeat business with past clients, your referral rate, your success level, your income, and your general level of happiness and satisfaction in your career.

Expertise. Your clients have hired you because they want to work with someone who knows more than they do. They expect you as their real estate agent to have a high level of expertise in contracts, the sales process, market conditions, and property values. Your clients expect you to know the geographic area including public schools, private schools, neighborhoods, local government issues and city services. They look to you for advice based on your expertise and experience. If you don't have the answers, they don't want you to make something up, they want you research it and get the accurate information for them.

Prospective clients come to you very informed and knowledgeable of the real estate market in their city and neighborhood. Buyers today spend hours scouring the internet for houses they are considering, while sellers are closely monitoring their local market by keeping tabs on other houses for sale in their neighborhood. Clients today will know a lot of information that in years past only real estate agents would know, and it's because this information is readily available on the internet.

To be successful as a real estate agent requires more knowledge than what you learn in real estate school. Take the time and effort to become an expert in your local market. Earlier I mentioned about becoming a doctor or lawyer and how specialized these professions are today. You have to think the same way as a real estate agent; you are the expert and you offer your advice and counsel to your clients based on your knowledge. The knowledge you attain takes time and effort and a focused learning so you continue to remain an expert in your field.

An Agent Who's Got My Back. Based on the comments I have compiled and on my own personal experience, I know that clients want someone who will protect, guide, advise and provide a high level of service throughout the entire sales process. In an ideal world, clients today want a level of caring for them from their real estate agent. They want to feel like they are the only client you have and get all of your attention.

Most people want an agent to represent their interests only, not both the buyer and the seller in the same transaction. Clients want you to be their agent and provide a level of representation that protects them and gets them the best terms and conditions for their deal. They also expect you to listen to what they want and give them choices based on their criteria, not yours.

Clients expect a high level of service. They want their real estate agent to communicate freely back and forth with them via phone, email, or text message. They want you to be available to answer their phone call if they call you. They don't want to be leaving voice mails all the time just to get you on the phone.

If you study and take away anything from this book it has to be what your client expects, wants and needs from you as their real estate agent. If you think about it, it's not a very complex job. You just do the best you can to service your clients with honesty based on your knowledge and expertise, produce positive results and then market yourself to new clients through your network of past clients and potential clients in the market place. It's a simple process, not easy, but simple if you just stay focused on what your clients expect, want and need from you.

Chapter 8
The Honesty Conflict

I would like to follow up on one of the real life examples I described in the "Introduction" of this book.

Your client says to you, "Wow, this is a great house, I really like it, and it has exactly the type of floor plan we want. What do you think of this neighborhood? Is it nice?" In your mind you are already struggling on how to respond. Here are your thoughts: "Man, I really need this deal, I haven't had a closing in three months. I thought these buyers were going to be easy. What do I say? Do I tell them the truth, or do I tell them what they want to hear since they like the house so much?"

It's important for you to understand how this process can happen with your clients. It happens so fast that often the client doesn't even realize what is happening.

In my example, you know it's not a nice neighborhood and the houses in the area have not appreciated much in the past ten years. Plus, you know there have been some crime problems recently with cars being broken into and personal items stolen.

Let's review your thought process on how you are going to respond: "Oh no, it is not a nice neighborhood. What am I going to say? I really need this deal and this house is perfect for them."

Here are three ways in which you can respond to your client. In this example your client does not know the area at all and is looking to you for advice based on your expertise.

- **First response**: "Um, it's an OK neighborhood. It's very close to the downtown, and the bus station we talked about is within walking distance, which I know is very important to you."

- **Second response**: "Yes, it's a very nice neighborhood. The trees are fully grown and a lot of the yards are well cared for. Plus, the bus station we talked about is within walking distance to the house."

- **Third response**: "Well, it's not one of the better neighborhoods in the area. They have had some theft crimes recently with people breaking into cars on the street. Plus, the elementary school has the lowest test scores in the area."

Think about how you might have responded. How do you feel about each of the responses? The second response is not honest at all based on what you know, and you are knowingly misleading your client. The third response is the most honest because it speaks directly to the problems in the neighborhood that you are aware of and which your client needs to know.

What do you think of the first response? It's OK, right? It's neutral and doesn't really say if the neighborhood is nice or bad. But, based on what your client is asking, you are not being honest with them because you are holding back information. You try to change the subject by talking about the proximity to the downtown area and the bus stop.

The most successful real estate agents today are the ones who are always honest with their clients and do not withhold any valuable or pertinent information. Now, if you as the real estate agent honestly did not know the neighborhood was bad or had recent crime issues then the first response would be fine. However, this demonstrates a lack of expertise on your behalf. You have not done your homework, and you do not know the details of the neighborhood. Even though you are being honest, this will come back to haunt you because your clients expect you to know this information as their real estate agent.

I have already told you a little bit about my career selling software in the world of high-tech. When I gave demonstrations on the software I was selling, my prospective customers did not expect me to know every single bit of functionality and features within the software. The software program was very complex and it was impossible for me to know every last thing about it, because I am not a software engineer.

Here's a joke I used to share with my sales colleagues back when we were selling software:

What is the difference between a used car salesman and a software salesman?

A used car salesman knows when he's lying.

Funny, isn't it? But this does not fly if you are a real estate agent. Your clients expect you to know **everything** about the properties, market data, and neighborhoods they are looking at. They expect you to tell them the truth and be honest with them. Your clients want to make their decision, often one of the biggest decisions in their lives, on how they will proceed based on the best information available. They don't want you to screen out information or paint an overly rosy picture for them. They want the truth.

Let's go back to our example. You decide to be honest and give the third response with the details you know about the problems and crime in the neighborhood. Your clients respond as follows:

"That is too bad about the recent crimes in the neighborhood, but we only have one car and it's always going to be in the garage. We don't have any kids, nor do we plan on having any, so the school issue is not important to us at all. Let's go take a look at the back yard again."

You did your duty in sharing the information they needed to know and they decided it was not important to them. Great! Now, don't you feel so much better as the real estate agent? Your clients really like the house. The biggest problem you were aware of is not a deterrent to them. You are on track to writing an offer on the house. Yes!

The conflict which goes on in your head when trying to decide if you should be completely honest with your clients happens so fast that most times you are not even aware of it. The best rule of thumb is to try and imagine yourself in your client's shoes. Say to yourself, "would I want to know this?" Usually you would want to know.

I suggest always being direct with your clients on issues. Stay on point and do not stray from the issue. I have been in sales for many years and I have seen inexperienced salespeople who just talk and talk. Sometimes it is out of nervousness, and sometimes out of a desire to control the situation. I have found over the years that the best way to stay in control of a conversation is to always be the one who is asking questions. It's best to just be quiet and let your clients absorb the situation and information without you blabbering on about things that are probably irrelevant.

To sum up, here are the advantages of always being honest with your clients:

1. Your relationships with your clients will be stronger and your clients will respect you more.
2. You will feel better about yourself because you know you are always being true to your clients and to yourself.
3. Once you have a successful closing with your clients, you will find they are very satisfied and grateful that you helped them through the entire process.

4. You will maintain good relationships with past clients because they feel good about you and the work you did for them.
5. You will receive more referrals from satisfied clients and more repeat business over the years because you have a reputation of always being honest with your clients.

It sounds simple to always be honest with your clients. However, I know from experience that it really takes a concerted effort on your behalf to master this skill. Be honest with your clients and yourself and you will enjoy your job more and earn more money in the long run.

Chapter 9
Market Analysis

Where do you plan on working as a real estate agent? Do you expect to work where you currently live? Or would you consider moving to a different geographic area? Regardless of where you end up, you have to do a thorough analysis of the market where you plan on working. This means looking at the following statistics:

- What is the average sales price and median price for the area where you plan on working?
- Are more people moving to your area compared to people moving out of the area?
- How is the job market currently and looking towards the future?
- What is the average number of days to a real estate contract?
- What are the inventory numbers for the cities you want to work in?

You should be able to get the answers to these questions from some of the real estate websites. I receive a monthly magazine online from my local Realtor Association and most of these statistics are included. Check with your local Realtor Association to see what data they have.

I suggest you build a model for this. The purpose is to try and identify what your average sales price is going to be for your transactions in the area you will be working in. This is helpful when you determine what your goal will be for total commissions in your first year, second year, third year and so on.

It would be ideal if you could hit the ground running and attain $100,000 in commissions your first year. Based on your research, say you determine the average sales price in your area is around $210,000. Work backwards to determine how many transactions you will need to close for the year to make your $100,000 in commissions. Commission rates vary since there is no standard commission rate for real estate agents.

If you only hit half of your target for commissions the first year, do not consider yourself a failure. You have to look at being a real estate agent as a long-term career. I will never forget my first year in sales after I graduated from college in the mid 1980s. I was selling turnkey computer systems which included software, hardware, support and training for small businesses. In my first year I made just under $18,000 for the entire year. That was pretty painful because I was working an average of 50 to 60 hours a week. I stuck with it and year after year my commissions and income increased. By the early 1990s I was consistently earning $80,000 to $100,000 a year.

Math can be boring stuff for some of us, but you have to take the time and effort to build a financial model so you know how many transactions you have to close each year. This knowledge will empower you to make the money you need, keep your business running, pay your bills, and take care of yourself and your family if you have one.

Here's a little secret about being a real estate agent. Usually, you will spend the same time and effort with a client regardless of the transaction amount, up to a certain point. In my experience I have found that I spend the same amount of time with a client buying a $225,000 house as I do with a client buying a $450,000 house. The sales process with each client is pretty much the same. The amount of time I spend with each client is identical. Yet the commission I make on the higher-priced house is about double what I make on the lower-priced house. This is very important for you to be aware of as you start your career. The similarities break down when you start selling to clients on the higher end, above $800,000 to $1,000,000. The reason why this example breaks down at this price point is that clients buying or selling a million dollar property have more specialized needs and challenges. In addition, the competition at this price point is very fierce.

And let's illustrate this point further. Let me ask you a question: would you rather close fifteen $225,000 transactions or ten $450,000 transactions, if the commission percentage was the same? A little math here: (15 x $225,000 = $3,375,000) and (10 x $450,000 = $4,500,000). You will obviously make more money in commissions with the ten $450,000 transactions, as well as working fewer hours.

Now you are probably thinking, "This is great! Now I see how to make money as a real estate agent: I need to focus on customers looking at high price points! Why would I ever want to work with a client in the $225,000 range?"

As I have said before, you have to always be thinking long-term. As I explained in my "honesty" chapter, trying to close what you see as that "big, important deal" right now, at the expense of everything else, can come back and bite you. In the long-term, the client currently in the $225,000 range will most likely one day buy a $450,000 house! Ideally, you should aim to work with clients in all price ranges. This way, the more clients you close, the more residual business you will receive in referrals and repeat business over time. Each year this keeps building and building, leading to what we refer to as "the snowball effect."

You might live in an area where the average sales price is in the $100,000 range. This should not discourage you. You simply build your business around this, knowing you will need to close at least 40 to 50 transactions a year to hit your income goals. Time management is absolutely critical when selling in a high transaction model such as this one. Your client list will grow, and you will find yourself increasing the number of transactions you are able to take on. As your career progresses you can then focus on increasing your average sales price per transaction.

As you move up in price with potential clients, you will begin to see a much higher level of competition with other top skilled agents. The challenge for us as real estate agents is that most times we do not choose who our clients are and we do not have any control over our average sales price per transaction. Still, through careful market analysis, goal setting and business planning we can achieve a level of control over our incomes.

Chapter 10
First Things First, You Need to Specialize

In today's highly competitive real estate market, with so many real estate agents all fighting for the same business, you have to be smart and set yourself apart from the competition. Today, the best way to do this is to specialize and focus on a portion of the market where you build your skills and expertise in that market segment. I will refer to this as your "niche." Think of your niche as the foundation of your business. It will not be all you do, but it is how you will set yourself apart from the crowd of other real estate agents.

To me this is one of the fun parts about being a real estate agent. You get to choose what you want to do based on your experience, skills, interests, competition, local market conditions and income goals. As I mentioned before, most people who become real estate agents are coming from other jobs or other life experiences. It's extremely rare to see someone go directly from college to a career in real estate, but it does happen. For those of you coming from a different industry, it would be ideal to try and capitalize on your previous work experience and leverage it for your real estate career.

Just before I became a real estate agent I was selling corporate housing services to companies and individuals locally. I was helping the Human Resource Departments of local companies when they were hiring out-of-state and sometimes out-of-country employees. It was a hard job and I did it for two and half years. While working there I learned all about the relocation industry. I really enjoyed helping the employees with their transition to a new area with their housing needs on a temporary basis. If they were interested in buying a home, I would refer them to real estate agents. This is when I realized I wanted to be a real estate agent myself. And today I specialize in relocation. I help clients move to my area of Colorado from out of state and all over the world, and I also assist them when they are leaving my area. I have built a good reputation in this niche and I market myself as a real estate agent who specializes in relocation.

Here is a checklist of factors to consider when choosing a niche:

1) **Competition:** Is there an established and strong real estate agent or agent team already working the niche you are considering? Ideally, find a niche where there are no established agents. Your chosen niche is a long-term commitment on your behalf and will require some ramp time. Once you start marketing and allocating your resources towards a niche, you are "branding" yourself. This becomes a sunk cost, and re-branding will be doubly expensive. You will want to stick with it and make it work in order for your business to be successful. Changing niches mid-stream would mean starting over and could stall or even kill your business entirely. If there are agents already in your desired niche, how strong are they? If they are not doing a good job and you see a window of opportunity, then go for it.

2) **Your Skill Set:** It's best to choose a niche where you already have experience and expertise. I know some agents who work a geographic territory where they have lived for a long time. "Horse Properties" is another great example of a niche. If you have experience riding and caring for horses and have lived or currently live on a horse property, this would be the perfect niche for you. Do you have strong financial and analytical skills? Then you might be a good fit for "Short Sales and Foreclosures" since the financial part of these transactions is very complex.

3) **Passion:** One of the keys for being successful in any niche is having a passion for that niche. If you live in a neighborhood or city and you love it, then your passion will shine through. Do you love boating? Are you an avid beach person? Depending on where you live you may want to focus on "Waterfront Properties."

4) **Average Sales Price:** You may be able to increase your average sales price per transaction based on the niche you choose. As I explained in Chapter 9, this can help increase your commissions and income on a yearly basis. For example, if your average sales price is $180,000 for your regular sales, and the niche you choose has an average sales price of $300,000, then your overall average sales price for all your deals will increase.

You never want to screen out clients based on sales price, but by proper planning you can choose a niche that can increase your income by increasing your average sales price for each of your sales closed.

5) **Growing or Dying Market:** Is the niche you are considering a growing or steady segment of your market? You don't want to choose a niche where you see demand dropping in the future. Where I live we have seen a steady decrease in demand and property values in mountain properties. If I were choosing a niche where I live I would avoid specializing in mountain properties because of this. How do you find out about this? Once you have access to your local property listing service you will be able to research and you will identify slow market areas. Your managing broker

will also be an excellent resource to give you advice in this area based on their experience and knowledge of the local market.

6) **Perceived Agent Value:** Will the clients in this niche recognize and appreciate your value based on your experience and expertise? You want to make sure you are working with clients who need you and want you. Tons of information is available online nowadays for consumers to investigate on their own. You want to make sure your niche is specialized in a way where your clients need your services.

For example, I have seen some hot neighborhoods where there are a lot of "For Sale By Owner" signs. This usually means that demand is so high from buyers that some sellers don't see any value in hiring a listing agent to work with them to sell their house. Brainstorm, and come up with reasons why your prospective buyers or sellers would need someone with your niche skills. These can become talking points for your first meeting with a new prospective client.

7) **Where are the builders building in your area?** Builders and developers do a lot of market research, and you can benefit from their work. Geographic areas that are currently being built up and new under-served markets suddenly being catered to are niches to consider. For example, are you seeing a lot of condos or assisted living communities spring up in what was formerly a strictly single-family detached market? Developers typically use good socioeconomic data to inform their decisions about what and where they will build. Look into these niches; chances are they will be growing in the future.

Here are some examples of successful niches you may want to consider:

- **Geographic Niche:** Choose a geographic location where you market yourself as the expert in that area. The geographic target you choose can be as big as a city or as small as a street or square block. This will be based on where you live and where you want to target. For example, in a large city like San Francisco or New York you can work a much smaller area because of higher population density. If you are in a rural area such as parts of the Midwest you can choose a county or even a good chunk of the state depending on density of population.

- **"Go Green" Niche:** Environmentally built and eco-friendly homes are gaining popularity. There are a number of real estate agents who have started to specialize in this area. Some parts of the country are more eco-friendly than others, so consider where you live.

- **Short Sales and Foreclosures Niche:** If you have a financial background or a head for numbers, specializing in distressed properties could be a good fit for you.

- **Buyer's Agent:** This is another niche that is very popular nowadays. You only work with buyers, offering them the highest level of service and representation. When you have a past client who wants to sell, instead of representing them yourself you refer them to another agent and collect a referral fee. I am not a big fan of this niche because I feel you leave money on the table over time by not doing listings for your past clients.

- **Divorce and Family Separations Niche:** Some real estate agents, especially those who have gone through a divorce, specialize in this niche. This requires a high level of patience and sensitivity when helping clients in these situations. You'll need to be emotionally strong to withstand the stressful process your client is going through.

A word of caution here: when I was selling corporate housing I came into contact with a number of people going through divorces and they were my most challenging clients. The reasons were numerous but the biggest issue is that people going through a divorce really don't know what they want to do from a housing standpoint because they are going through so much stress with their divorce. The housing issues are secondary to them and they end up changing their minds on issues quite a bit.

- **Downsizing Niche:** Another good niche to consider based on the demographics where you will be working is helping people move from their big family house to a smaller home. The Baby Boomers are all getting older and they need to downsize once their kids are out of school and college. This niche again requires someone with high "emotional intelligence."

- **Luxury Homes and Neighborhoods Niche:** Real estate agents who live in luxury homes themselves do best in this niche. They understand the special needs, desires and considerations of clients who are buying homes greater than one million dollars and upwards. If you fit this profile, then this is a good niche to consider.

- **Relocation Niche:** Clients moving to a new area or leaving their current area have special needs as well. Their timeframes are compressed and they usually have hard and fast deadlines to meet. The real estate agent specializing in the relocation niche requires a high level of organization and knowledge of the local area. When representing the relocating seller, this niche requires an ability to interface and report to any relocation companies involved in the transaction. I enjoy this niche because it fits very well with my skill set. I have lived in my area most of my life so I know the cities, neighborhoods and schools on a personal level. I have corporate sales experience and can relate well with clients and all parties involved in this niche.

- **Senior Communities Niche:** In Colorado we have seen a number of new Senior Housing Communities developed and built in the past ten years. As I mentioned before, watching what the developers do can often signal a trend. In this case, a large segment of the population, the Baby Boomers, are retiring and downsizing. This can be an exciting niche as housing developments for people 55 and over compete for this business. Some of these communities are pretty amazing in what they offer!

- **Horse and Farm Properties Niche:** Depending on where you live this might be a good option for you, especially if you have horses or grew up around horses. Check out your area! Most states in the U.S. and provinces in Canada have horse and farm properties.

- **Investor Buyers Niche:** You work with investors helping them identify properties which fit their portfolio. To be successful in this niche, you need to be able to identify value properties for your clients. A high level of professionalism and an analytical approach is best. Investors will not buy a property based on emotion; it's an investment to them so they will be more direct and matter of fact in their negotiations.

- **Property Management Niche:** You receive a percentage of the monthly rent of properties you manage on behalf of property owners. This is not a traditional real estate agent model if you focus exclusively on property management, but it does have a higher level of security when starting your career. I see a lot of agents who start in property management and then transition into an Investor Buyers niche.

- **For Sale By Owner (FSBO) and Expired Listings Niche:** You focus on listings by prospecting FSBOs and expired listings. As I mentioned, FSBO properties can be difficult because the seller is basically stating that he or she sees no value in hiring a listing agent to help them sell their property. Expired listings mean that the contracted listing agent has not sold the home in the amount of time in their contract, and the agent / seller relationship has come to an end. Sellers may be upset, asking whose fault it is that the home hasn't sold. I know a lot of real estate agents who focus on FSBOs and expired listings, but I feel you need to be more experienced to do this successfully. It might be a bit of a challenge in your first year.

The list I have included is just a summary of possibilities. As we move towards the future we are going to see more and more niche markets in real estate. The key to making a niche work for you is to choose one when you start and stick with it. When we discuss your marketing plan you will see how your niche is an integral part of your marketing campaign.

Chapter 11
Choose the Right Company and Stay There!

The company you choose to work at initially and the skills you acquire while there are some of the biggest factors in determining your long-term success as a real estate agent. I have given this chapter a lot of thought, and I believe this is the most important and the most difficult decision you make after you get your real estate license.

I suggest when you are considering companies, you contact real estate agents that you know and ask them which companies would be a good fit for you. If you don't know many agents then I suggest you look online for real estate companies that have a strong presence locally and then either call and ask for the managing broker or stop by their offices. It is completely acceptable for you to make a phone call or a visit and you won't be treated harshly at all.

When you find a company that you are interested in, then make sure to meet and talk with the owner or managing broker to get a feel for how they do business. Make sure you choose a company that fits your personality and how you want to do business. Would you want to be a customer of this company?

I chose RE/MAX because it was the perfect fit for me based on my experience, skills and the niches I had chosen to focus on: Relocation and First Time Home Buyers. Looking back, I didn't do much research myself before choosing RE/MAX. I knew they had a strong presence locally combined with a strong national brand which did help me with my Relocation and First Time Buyer clients because they knew of RE/MAX as a reputable company.

When I first started, RE/MAX usually only hired people who had a least three to five years of experience as a real estate agent and a proven track record of sales. My first managing broker, Dan Johnson, saw something in me based on my corporate sales experience and my knowledge of the local area even though I had only just started out as a real estate agent.

The business model of the company or the "team" you work for is very important. You should ask what the commission structure will be beforehand so you can get an idea of how you will achieve your income goals. The commission structure for me at RE/MAX was the following when I started: I paid approximately $1,100 a month to my RE/MAX office, which is RE/MAX Alliance. On an annual basis I paid a fee of approximately $350 to RE/MAX Corporate. When I closed a deal I then received 100% of the commissions I made as a result of my sales.

I was a little nervous when I started because, in reality, I was the owner of my business. I had real overhead where I had to write a check to my office each month, just like a rent check. In addition, I had to pay all of the other related business expenses myself, such as for sale signs, business cards, letterhead, and envelopes. I am proud to say that I have never missed nor skipped a monthly payment to my office in the 10+ years I have worked there.

If you don't have money in savings to carry you through the first year, you might consider joining a company or team where you are on what is called a split model. The commissions you receive are split between you and your employer. The split can be anywhere from 25% to 50% on average. For example, if you receive a $5,000 commission on a transaction, your employer would then pay out to you your share based on the split percentage you have in place. If the split is 50% then you would receive $2,500, for example. The split model is good for people starting out because you will not have any overhead in terms of desk fees like I did when I started out on my own. The split percentage rate is lowered over time, once you have worked for a few years and have generated good sales results.

You could also start out as a licensed assistant for another real estate agent during your first year. You would make a nominal salary supporting and servicing another agent. This would give you a way to learn more about the business without taking on all the risk of going out on your own. This is an effective starting point for some people, especially if you do not have much sales experience, because your income would not be predicated on your own results. The agent you work for takes on that responsibility and pays you out of their commissions.

Regardless of whether you start on a split model or as a licensed assistant, try to find a company where you would want to continue working once you are completely on your own. That way the brand recognition you build will carry through when you go out on your own as an individual real estate agent.

If I were starting out today and I had minimal sales experience I would take this career path:

- My first year I would work as a licensed assistant for another agent who worked at XYZ Real Estate.
- My next two years I would work as a buyer's agent on a team who worked at XYZ Real Estate.
- My fourth year I would go out on my own and be my own agent and work at XYZ Real Estate.

Staying at the same company shows stability for you and helps brand you as a real estate agent. Your personal network, or "sphere of influence," will begin to link your name with your company as they continue to see your name associated with the same company. When your company runs advertising, you will benefit from it because your sphere will think of you.

There are a lot of excellent real estate companies out there. Take the time to research them, especially those who are major players in your area. You should be able to identify the strong companies in your area very easily.

Choose the company where you want to be, and stay there forever. I am only half kidding! I feel it is very important and shows stability and dedication when you are able to stay with one company for many years. Clients want to work with a person who is stable and dedicated.

A friend of mine is a sales and marketing target for a lot of real estate agents. He is constantly bombarded with marketing materials from real estate agents. He told me recently that many of the agents who contact him seem to be constantly changing companies. He notices and remembers when agents work at one company for a year or two, move to another company briefly, and then change companies again. He said when he sees this he really questions the integrity and skills of these agents. They come across as unstable as they continue to change companies. Did they fail to hit their numbers? Are they having interpersonal issues in the office? Are they any good at being a real estate agent? These are the questions my friend asks himself. When they contact him for the twentieth time, they say the new company they work for is the best, and then they ask my buddy to do business with them…again. My friend says this seems to be very common among the agents who are targeting him as a prospective customer.

What is the ideal real estate company for you? When I look to the future, I see the following in real estate companies:

1. **Choose a company that will enable you to work from home and the office.** Real estate is a 24/7 job, especially when you are negotiating deals on a weekend. I have a workstation in my home and I have a cube with a

desk at my office. You don't need a personal office for yourself at the company where you work. All you need is a cube or a desk in a bullpen.

2. **Internet connectivity and a good printer are a must**. Many real estate agents are now able to do contracts via email with electronic signatures. This is great because it's reducing the amount of paper we go through on a daily basis. You need access to a good printer for printing out contracts, MLS sheets, and other business related documents.

3. **Nice conference rooms are important** so you have a place to meet with clients.

4. The company you work for needs to have **a professional looking office environment**.

5. **A professional office staff** who provide support to you on your contracts and paperwork.

6. Most companies now are **outsourcing the scheduling of showings** on listings and I see this trend to continue.

7. **Look for a company with strong brand recognition**. Ideally, your company will be a household name, have a strong brand and a good reputation in the market where you will be working. Make sure your prospective company does advertising to promote its brand through both traditional advertising methods and social media.

8. **A strong web presence is a must** and will be more important as we move to the future. The company you work for should have its own web page with staff or resources dedicated to SEO (Search Engine Optimization). It would be awesome if you could receive real, qualified leads from the web that you convert into closings.

I see a lot of real estate companies today that are struggling financially because they are not adapting to the new ways of doing business. The old style, brick and mortar companies with high overhead costs are going to have to dramatically change how they do business or they will continue to lose market share and eventually go out of business. As I mentioned before, the demographics are changing in the real estate industry. The Baby Boomer real estate agents will be retiring soon. The new generation of real estate agents will not be attracted to real estate companies who stick to the old ways of doing business.

My final point about choosing where you will work is to consider the skills you will be acquiring as you start your career. In a traditional job we receive two tangible forms of compensation: a paycheck and job skills. Think back to a job you had when you were younger. I remember my days of working at our family restaurant during my high school and college years. I didn't make much money but I did acquire valuable work skills which have served me well in my career. At the restaurant, I learned management skills, organization skills, a strong work ethic, conflict resolution skills, customer service skills, advertising and marketing, and cooking skills. If you were to visit our house for a Sunday brunch I could make you a mean breakfast, even today. Even though I did not make much money in terms of a paycheck while working at our restaurant, I acquired valuable skills which have helped me be successful in my professional career after I graduated from college.

The same applies to your real estate career. The first few years you will need to pay your dues, especially if you have little or no experience in sales or real estate. Keep previewing homes, host open houses for your colleagues, keep writing the blogs, keep taking continuing education classes, keep practicing, keep role playing, keep reading the books and listening to the tapes. Think of it as an apprenticeship because you will be learning about the real estate profession and learning the skills required to be successful as a real estate agent.

Chapter 12
Mentors and Training

Once you start out in your real estate career, pursue opportunities to be trained and mentored. This could prove more challenging than it sounds! Many jobs come prepackaged with orientation, training courses, and even mentoring programs. But one of the things you will find as a real estate agent is that other agents in your office will not be so cooperative in helping you. You may not believe it at first, but the root of this is that they view you as competition.

I remember early on in my career, I innocently asked another agent in my office where he was getting his clients from. He immediately clammed up on me and said, "no one likes working with a secret agent." I still don't know what he meant and I was surprised at his response. It was the last time I asked any of my colleagues in my office for advice or help.

I suggest you do what Napoleon Hill did. Mr. Hill is the author of the book **Think and Grow Rich.** He interviewed the successful people of his time, and then wrote his book based on the interviews. It was a simple idea, but it is now recognized as the foundational book of the personal development movement in the 20th Century! So search out other successful real estate agents locally and nationally, as well as through networking. If the agent is local, ask if they can go out to lunch with you, your treat of course. Then over lunch, talk to them. Learn about what they did initially in their career as a real estate agent to get going. Ask them what they do today to remain successful.

I remember years ago a buddy and I were able to have lunch with Larry Wilson, co-author of the book *The One Minute Salesperson*. Larry was someone that I respected and I wanted to emulate, so my friend and I asked him to lunch. Our discussion that day has always stuck with me. I learned a lot from that one lunch meeting that I would have otherwise never have learned. On a national level, you can meet other successful real estate agents through networking and social media. Ask them if they will be willing to take a phone call from you. Be prepared with at least five good questions. Here are a few to get you started:

- How long did it take you to get your real estate business going?
- What would you do differently in your early days knowing what you know today?

- What is your area of specialty or niche? How did you choose it? Or did it choose you?
- What advice can you give me as I start my career in real estate?
- What do you enjoy most about being a real estate agent?

You can think of other questions to ask, but use these as a starting point when meeting with successful real estate agents for lunch or chatting on the phone. If you find one good mentor it will be invaluable to your career. Don't give up! Keep asking other agents around town for their time. Eventually you will find someone who is willing to help.

If a new agent approached me today and asked me to lunch, I'd be very happy to share my experiences and insights with them. I clearly remember how it was when I started out in sales and I did have a few mentors along the way help me.

I recommend you join your local Realtor board because they offer a lot of excellent real estate classes. I have been very pleased with my local Realtor board and the classes they offer each year. You will also find that local title and mortgage companies offer excellent training classes.

There are a number of designations you can receive as a result of continuing education as a real estate agent. Here are a few to consider:

- Accredited Buyer's Representative / ABR
- Certified Residential Specialist® / CRS
- NAR's Green Designation / GREEN
- Graduate, REALTOR® Institute / GRI
- Seniors Real Estate Specialist®, SRES
- e-PRO
- Short Sales & Foreclosures Resource / SFR
- Certified Negotiation Expert (CNE)

Evaluate some of these designations in relation to your local market. Your managing broker can offer you advice in this area.

Some other strategies for learning and mentoring:

1. Ride along with another agent during a house showing tour with buyers.
2. Sit in on a listing presentation with another agent in a different territory.
3. Role-play different sales situations with another agent in your office. Take turns being the real estate agent and the customer. I have found that I learn more about how to be effective when I am the customer. This gives me the opportunity to really see and experience how they feel.

4.   Sit and observe an open house that another agent is hosting.
5.   Learn about the home inspection process by asking another agent to let you observe how they resolve one.
6.   The next time you are traveling out of state, check out the local real estate market. Visit a few open houses and take a look at what is available. I've done this a few times and it's very powerful to see how it feels to be a customer. It gives you the opportunity to see how other agents around the country host open houses.
7.   Write a Home Buying Guide for your buyers. I remember doing this when I started out and it was a lot of work, but it was very valuable because it helped me understand the buying process better. It even helped me develop my presentation skills because I was more confident with the material.

We all need to keep ourselves sharp by attending continuing education classes. I always enjoy getting a fresh perspective on important topics and challenges we face as real estate agents.

Rant alert! Here's my take on the national "coaches" and "trainers" in the real estate industry. You don't need them! You can be successful on your own without making these coaches and trainers richer. In my opinion these people are more entertainers than actual trainers. For some of them, it's been 20-30 years since they were a real estate agent. Others have never actually sold real estate! These coaches and trainers are excellent at selling their books, videos, coaching programs and sales paraphernalia to real estate agents, but when was the last time they were in the trenches actually helping buyers and sellers?

What I *have* seen from most of the coaches and trainers out there is the same old tired and antiquated methods of the past, including things such as:

"Maintain a positive attitude."
"Call or talk to ten people a day about buying or selling a house."
"Call on expired listings."
"Do pop-by's on past clients."
"Handwrite ten cards a day to your sphere."
"Stay focused and work hard."
"If you believe you can do it, then you can do it."

Most of these coaches and trainers are just regurgitating the same thing year after year. They may spice it up with new stories and funny anecdotes, but you are not getting anything new or earth-shattering for your money. The coaching programs, online courses and seminars are very expensive, and you are promised the moon. You are given a hard sell on these training programs and many fall into the trap believing it will actually help and improve their sales results. They won't! Trust me. I have attended a few over the years and I always enjoy the part when we repeat the morning mantras:

"Today is a good day." "I am good at what I do." "I like myself."

What I find interesting in a lot of these seminars is that I don't learn anything new. It's more of a feel-good session than anything.

You may even have seasoned agents tell you that you have to spend your hard-earned money on these programs, but I say it's not worth it! Many real estate sales seminars cost thousands of dollars, plus your travel expenses. Don't fall for any of these. They are not worth it, and some of them are even scams. Just say no! I cannot wholeheartedly recommend *any* national coaches or trainers that are worth the investment. You are better off saving your money, reading some good sales books and learning from others that you respect.

I have already mentioned several books that I have found invaluable. A quick disclosure: I am not receiving any commission nor do I have any business relationship with these publishers or authors. They simply have been effective for me and made a positive impact on my sales results:

- *SPIN Selling* by Neil Rackham

- *The One Minute Salesperson* by Spencer Johnson

- *The New Conceptual Selling: The Most Effective and Proven Method for Face-to-Face Sales Planning* by Heiman, Tuleja, Miller and Coghlan

- *Take Charge of Your Life* by Jim Rohn. This is an audio series that helped me a lot in my early years. It's a six-CD set and you can buy it online. I highly recommend this particular tape series!

The Kindle app from Amazon is a great resource for people. You can buy an e-book which has real value to you for only $9.99 or even less sometimes. As of this writing, most Kindle books are at this price point. In addition, there are other resources for e-books on iTunes and Google, which are very exciting for people looking to improve themselves personally.

Chapter 13
What Do Real Estate Agents Really Sell?

I'm going to make a bold statement, but one that you should take to heart. As real estate agents, we don't sell houses. The houses sell themselves based on the individual buyers' needs and their buying criteria. The reality is that buyers and sellers are both much more informed today because of the Internet and the information available there. A lot of real estate agents don't want to talk about this because they feel that if they're not selling houses, they are out of a job. So what do we sell as real estate agents if we don't sell houses? We really sell ourselves. We are the product; we sell our service and more specifically our knowledge and expertise. Our product knowledge is the geography we cover, the contracts we write and our mastery of the entire sales process on behalf of our clients.

In my early years of selling I listened to a lot of "motivational tapes" and one of the speakers I really enjoyed was Jim Rohn. Here's one of his best quotes: "To have more than you've got, become more than you are." It's a very powerful statement. If you want to sell more and earn more commissions each year then you need to improve yourself as the product. This is a different way of viewing yourself as a real estate agent, but one that will motivate you to get better and become more valuable to your clients. It will lead you to continually attract more clients based on how much value you bring to them. I'll say it again: *"To have more than you've got, become more than you are."*

Imagine that you are a product and ask yourself the following questions:

- How well do you present?
- How well do you speak?
- How well do you listen?
- Do you ask the right questions at the right time?
- What type of message does the office you work in present to the clients who visit you there?
- How well does your company present itself to the public?
- Do you have an effective personal website?
- How well do you know the geographic areas you cover?
- How well do you know the sales statistics in your area?

- How well do you know the real estate trends in your area?
- How well do you know the public and private schools in your area?
- How well do you know your contracts and disclosure forms?
- How are your negotiation skills?
- Are you a likable person? Do you get along well with others?
- Do you feel good about yourself? Do you like yourself?
- Do you have energy throughout the day?

Think about how you are viewed by your clients. Put yourself in their shoes. If you needed a real estate agent, would you hire yourself? Unlike the unproductive sales tactics we discussed earlier, spending time improving yourself as the product and focusing on these questions will help create that long, successful career you want.

Local Geographic Knowledge

Our clients look to us as experts in the local geography where we work. It's important for us to be well versed on the cities we cover, the different neighborhoods, the public and private schools, the sales statistics for the area, parks and open space, transportation, city government issues and any other information that would be useful to a resident.

It would be ideal if we lived and worked in the same city, but often this is not the case. As real estate agents it is crucial that we take the time and effort to study each area that we cover. Of course, there is a lot of information available on the Internet for us to review. But I think it is best to physically go to the cities and view the homes prior to your meetings or tours so you are prepared. I will always do a preview of the homes in a neighborhood I'm not that familiar with prior to a listing presentation or a buying tour. It is extra work, but it does pay off for me. This type of preparation gives me firsthand and recent exposure to the neighborhoods and streets where I will be going and gives me excellent talking points when I meet with my client.

Expertise in Real Estate Procedure

Another important area where clients need our expertise as real estate agents—and part of what they are buying when they work with us if "we are the product"—is our knowledge of contracts, disclosures, foreclosures, short sales and the steps sellers and buyers have to go through to reach a successful closing. With the exception of New Jersey, every state in the United States requires real estate licensees to earn continuing education in order to maintain their real estate license. The training available for contracts and sales process is excellent nowadays, and most local real estate agent boards and associations do a great job at keeping real estate agents educated. The bare minimum for us as professionals is to make sure we attend the appropriate number of training classes and get the necessary credits to maintain our license. Every year the contracts we use get updated with new clauses and legal changes, which makes the update courses and contracts classes even more crucial to attend on a regular basis. This is a big part of your value to your clients since most of them do not have any knowledge of the real estate contracts and disclosures, nor will most of them take the time to research this type of information on their own.

Don't Forget, It is a Sales Job

Being a successful real estate agent means you have to be a successful salesperson; the two go hand in hand. There is the rare person who is just a natural; the minute they get into real estate they do well without any formal sales training. But most of us need to take the time to consciously study a foundation of selling skills.

Some real estate companies do offer excellent in-house sales training, mentoring, and coaching programs. Many times there is also training available via video on your company's Intranet. By all means, take advantage of these if they are available. There are tons of people out there selling their "magic" real estate agent sales training programs, but they are often expensive. Frankly, I have been surprised at the lack of good sales training for real estate agents that is available today.

Being good at sales isn't a personality trait; it's a learned profession. I was lucky because prior to becoming a real estate agent I was in the world of high tech sales selling software. I attended many (sometimes too many!) sales training seminars over the years. I was able to pick up some great sales techniques, strategies, and habits that have served me well and made me a successful real estate agent. Here are some of the best I have learned which apply to being a real estate agent:

"The Shark Principle"

A sales metaphor that is very easy to remember and especially applicable to your career in real estate is one I will call "the shark principle." It's a known fact that if a shark stops swimming he will die; a shark's gills are simply unable to process oxygen if he stops moving, so he suffocates. How does this apply to sales in real estate? From the first time we meet our client, we need to be moving forward towards our goal of getting under contract and then to a successful closing. There are many steps involved with helping our client get through this process, so everything we do needs to move us toward this goal. If your client is not moving forward on a deal, the deal will die just as a shark dies when it stops moving forward.

For example, let's say you are helping a buyer and you go out a few times to view some homes. The client then informs you that she will be taking a "break" from viewing homes. This is not a good sign, and there might be an excellent reason why the client wants to stop. If you don't know the reason why or what it will take for your buyer to become active again, this will bring the deal to a standstill. According to "the shark principle," one way to avoid certain death in this scenario would be to get your client to commit to scheduling the next home viewing tour at some time in the future, let's say three weeks out. Doing so is a delay, but not one you should worry about because you are moving the sale forward.

As a salesperson you need to be closing on the next step of the sales process just like a shark that is always swimming forward. Your ability to anticipate what should happen next, get the right information from your client and get a commitment to move forward to the next step will win you respect and help you close more business. After all, your clients are working with you because they want to close on that house, too! Here again you are getting what you want by helping your client get what he or she wants.

My record for number of homes viewed with a buyer is 110 homes, but I knew I wasn't wasting my time with this particular couple. It was obvious that the buyers had very specific criteria for a house and it was just taking us longer than usual to find the right fit. How did I know for sure I would close them? I remember we took a break in August because it was just too hot for one of the buyers to be driving around in a car. We scheduled right then and there to get back to looking at homes again in September, so the break didn't concern me. I had closed them on the next step and we were moving forward, which saved me a lot of stress and uncertainty.

Closing on the next step, or "the shark principle" sounds simple but it does take practice and discipline. It is a sales skill you need to develop and hone over time. If not, your clients will lose interest, go into a holding pattern, or find another real estate agent to work with. In addition, the certainty that comes with "the shark principle" is the only way you will consistently be able to create an accurate sales forecast, another key to your success.

Sales Forecasting and the "Pipeline" Theory

Prior to becoming a real estate agent, in all my sales jobs I was required to submit a sales forecast to management. As an individual real estate agent, you are effectively running your own company, so disciplining yourself to create an accurate sales forecast with opportunities in every stage of the "sales pipeline" is very important, since it directly affects your personal bottom line.

There are all kinds of sales forecast models, but the one I use as a real estate agent is very straightforward. I keep a spreadsheet and track active buyers, active listings, and buyers and listings which are identified but not yet active, and future business. I set a commission goal for the year and I assign all of the corresponding commissions in dollars to my active and future clients. This allows me to see how much commission I will make based on my current active business and also by what could happen in future business. I can make conservative estimates, based on past performance, that a certain percentage of these transactions will not happen, and I can take steps to fill in my pipeline with more business early to avoid surprises late in the year.

No matter how optimistic I am about a certain deal or group of deals, I always calculate that the entire dollar amount in my forecast will not happen. There are always unforeseen circumstances in sales, and it's important to be realistic. Formal sales training or not, we all know that nothing is certain in life and no deal should ever be forecasted as a 100 percent sure thing until it is closed.

If you don't have a sales forecast program or pipeline spreadsheet set up already, I highly recommend you put one together. It's a simple exercise, but important that you know at all times where your business is at and where you need to be focusing to build your pipeline. For example, let's say your forecast shows you have a lot of active buyers and active listings, but you have no future clients identified. This means your business is going to be slow after all of your closings because you will effectively be starting over. A sales cycle can take months for an active buyer or listing, but good pipeline management will help prevent the valleys that often occur after the peaks in our business.

"Nice" Doesn't Cut It

A trap that we all fall into as real estate agents is equating being "nice" to being a successful real estate agent. There are a lot of really nice real estate agents out there who are struggling and not making deals happen because they don't understand the true nature of sales. Don't get me wrong, I am not saying that being a jerk is the answer either. You can and should be nice and pleasant to your clients, but you have to be so much more. You have to be focused on helping your clients make a good decision, and determined to get your clients to the closing table successfully.

As real estate agents, we have a responsibility to tell our clients some things they do not want to hear. A good example is when we are sitting down with clients to discuss getting their house ready to list and sell. These can be emotional meetings because sellers are very attached to their homes. They may resist doing what we recommend, even when it is in their best interest. I remember one time I was talking to a seller about all of the family pictures he had in his house. There were a lot of pictures, they were everywhere, and I was very firm in explaining that all of these pictures had to be taken down. The seller and I had a good exchange of ideas on the subject, but I drew a line in the sand and held my ground because this issue was not negotiable. In this situation I was not very "nice" to the seller, but I was helping him get his house sold.

There are also plenty of examples of being firm with buyers in order to help them make the best purchasing decision possible. I remember once I was taking a buyer to view homes. We visited a house that was just perfect for her. It was really nice on the inside, had the floor plan she wanted, and the house fit most of her criteria. But the house backed to a highway. This wasn't your typical busy street, but a highway where cars were zipping by really fast. The house had been on the market for a long time, much longer than the average time on the market for that area. I had to be very firm and explain to her that this house was not a good fit because of the highway behind it. I told her she might be okay living there with the highway, but reminded her of what it did to resale value. What would happen when it came time for her to sell the house? We had a good debate on the subject but I stuck to my position and let her know my thoughts: this was not going to be a wise investment for her. The decision was ultimately up to her, but I wanted her to fully understand what she would be getting into.

After a few days she emailed me and said that I was right. She thanked me for being so honest with her. This is where we, as real estate agents, can set ourselves apart. Again, it reminds us that we are not selling houses, we are selling our expertise. People will want to work with us and refer us to friends because we help them make wise decisions. To me it didn't matter that I was right or wrong about this particular house. I wanted my buyer to be educated and informed about her choice. I wasn't simply trying to "close" her so I could make my commission quickly. She ended up with a much better house in the end and was very happy and appreciative towards me.

At times, being a real estate agent is similar to being a parent. We have to tell our kids what they don't want to hear because it is our job to take care of them and keep them safe. Replace "kids" with "clients" in that sentence and apply it to your work. Being a real estate agent is about more than just making a sale. We are helping our clients with their lives because the house we live in is a big part of who we are as people.

I never feel shy or timid about being firm with my clients, because I can always refer back to the principles I learned in the book *The One Minute Salesperson.* My purpose as a real estate agent is to help my clients get what they want and need. I am always anticipating the future and using my experience to make sure my clients are making a good long-term decision in the purchase or sale of their home.

Asking the Right Questions
A few quick tips from the book *SPIN Selling* by Neil Rackham. This is hands down the best book I have read on the mechanics of selling, because it teaches you how to ask questions specific to your product or service. In *SPIN Selling*, the initial meeting we have with our client is called a "needs-analysis." This meeting develops our understanding of our client's needs and defines how we are going to help meet them. As real estate agents, we can set the stage for our relationship with our client in this meeting by being prepared and by asking effective questions.

One of the most powerful questions we can ask during the "needs analysis," according to Neil Rackham, is the "need-payoff" question. Here are some examples of "need-payoff" questions for real estate agents:

- How do you think I can help you as your real estate agent? What prompted you contact me?
- What benefits do you see from owning your own home?
- Why is it important to you that you sell your home now?

A "need-payoff" question accomplishes two things. First, it gets the customer to focus on the solution rather than the problem. Second, it gets the customer to articulate the benefits of your product or service. Research shows that "need-payoff" questions create a positive effect between the customer and salesperson and are linked to successful relationship sales models.

The key is getting your client to tell you the reasons why they want to buy or sell a home from their perspective. When a client tells you how you can help them as their real estate agent, this further locks them in with you personally. They will see you as their real estate agent before you even get started.

Pick up a copy of *SPIN Selling*. You will not be disappointed; this book will help you ask better questions and help you serve your clients more effectively.

The Value of Effective Preparation
Walking into a meeting with a client and "winging it" without truly being prepared is a bad habit we often fall into as real estate agents. Maybe we have done a particular type of meeting so many times that we don't feel the need to prepare, or perhaps we don't see the value in preparation. But let me assure you that when we fail to prepare we are doing a disservice to our clients and ourselves. Preparation, from studying effective questioning techniques to touring a city or community prior to meeting with a client, is what successful real estate professionals do.

One habit I learned early on in my sales career is the value of role-playing. For some reason, as we get older we have a high resistance to this exercise, and I'm not sure why. It is valuable, because you actually get to practice what you are going to do and say, so you are prepared. The best way to make that important first impression is to be fully prepared. Given the state of our industry today, we can't afford to make a single bad impression.

I had lunch with a friend of mine the other day. She asked me why I felt I was successful as a real estate agent. The first thought that came to my mind is that I put in the work to be prepared, so I am competent in what I do. The discussion with my friend made me realize how much work I actually do in preparing for my meetings with my clients, and how important it is. Good preparation allows me to be confident in answering the straightforward questions my clients ask, which builds their confidence in me as their real estate agent.

Some examples of good preparation:

- A few days prior to a home tour in an area you are not completely familiar with, go out and preview all of the homes. You should drive around the city and have lunch there to give you a better feel for the city and the neighborhoods.
- Do a "Competitive Market Analysis" for a seller and present it to them at the first meeting you have. Even if they are not committed to listing at this time, it will give them a good idea about how their house fits into the market.
- Prepare all of the materials you will present at a first meeting with a buyer at least two days in advance. The day before and the day of the meeting, review your notes and the questions you will ask so you will be more effective in the meeting.
- Prior to a meeting with a referral, talk with or email the person who referred them. Find out how they know each other and thank them for the referral.

Chapter 14
Live in the World of Reality, Not Hope

Years ago, I was manager of a regional inside sales team at Rogue Wave Software. Part of my responsibilities included preparing the sales forecasts I prepared for the management team. This involved sitting down with each sales representative for a pipeline review. My job was to use my best judgment to figure out what was a real deal in their pipeline and what was not a real deal. I would then include the real deals—the ones that we could count on to close by the end of the month—in my regional forecast for upper management.

In the pipeline review, I asked the reps questions about where each deal stood, what the next step was, and the commitment made by the customer about placing a purchase order. It was an interesting exercise, and I learned that the following could be what I will call "red flag" statements:

- "I talked to the purchasing agent last week. He said he was working on it, so I hope we'll get the purchase order by the end of the month."
- "I talked to my contact on the project team. She said she submitted her request up to her manager and then it will go to purchasing. I hope to get the order soon."
- "The tech lead gave the approval for our software, but it now has to go to the project manager for approval. I did get a commitment from her last week. She said she would approve and then send to purchasing. I really hope to get the order by the end of the month because we have worked hard on this with our technical staff."

They all sound pretty good, right? But you may have noticed there is one key word in each statement from the reps: the word "hope." Whenever I heard a rep tell me they "hoped" they would get the deal soon, I knew they had not received a full commitment from their contacts. Salespeople are notorious for having "happy ears," which means they are always optimistic, and always believe what the customer says about an order coming through. Over time, I worked with the team and taught them how to differentiate between a deal they were "hoping" for and a real deal they could bank on. You can do this by qualifying or screening the customer to make sure he or she has both the motivation and the means to place an order. How does this apply to our careers in real estate? Well, listen to yourself the next time you are talking to a colleague, family member or friend about one of your deals. Here are some things you might hear yourself say:

- "I took some buyers out this past weekend. We had a good tour and I think I connected well with them. We saw a bunch of houses, it was our first time out together, and I really hope they call me back so we can schedule our next tour."
- "I've got this tough listing. The sellers are really difficult because they have the house priced way too high given the market. I really hope I can get it sold by the end of the listing period."
- "I was holding an open house this Sunday. I had a lot of people attend. I met one buyer and we got along well. We chatted for a while about the market and I gave her my card. I really hope she calls me."

You get the idea. We do it to ourselves all the time. We live in the world of hope. The biggest time waster for real estate agents is spending time with unqualified clients and "hoping" they will become qualified. We can avoid this trap if we continually use the "shark principle" I discussed earlier. We need to always be closing on the next step, getting a commitment, and also qualifying the client to make sure they are really an active buyer or serious about listing their house.

Qualifying Clients
For buyers, save yourself valuable time and headaches by always qualifying on the following:

- **Means.** Do they have the means? Financially, are they in a position to buy a house?
- **Motivation**. Why do they want to buy a house? What is driving their decision? Is there an impending event that is motivating their purchase?
- **Timeline.** When do they need to do this by? If there is an impending event, when will it happen? Could anything change?
- **Choice of real estate agent**. How can you as their real estate agent help them? Why are they choosing you? Make sure there is a fit here and that you are providing what they expect. Once you start on this venture together, you want to make sure they are committed to you, and you to them, as their real estate agent. If this is the case, you will be headed towards a closing together.

For sellers, the questions are similar:

- **Motivation**. Why do they want to sell their house? Where do they want to go? Are they planning to move up to a larger house or different neighborhood? Do they want to move out of the area, or move down to a smaller house?
- **Means**. Do they have the means to do what they want to do?
- **Timeline**. Is there an impending event such as a job transfer or relocation? When will this happen, and could anything change?
- **Choice of real estate agent**. Again, are you as the real estate agent a good fit with the sellers? Ask them how you as their real estate agent can help them. Are you able to provide what they expect?

Giving your clients some kind of assignment or task is a great way to qualify clients. If they are actively following up and participating in the sales process, you are more likely to have a qualified client on your hands. This is important and worth repeating: if your client is **not** participating in the sales process by completing the assignment or task, then most likely they are either not really interested or not really qualified. Having an interest and being qualified go together. There are a lot people interested in buying a house, but they have to be qualified to buy.
Here are some examples of tasks or assignments to give to buyers to gauge interest and further qualify them:

- Have them contact a lender to get pre-qualified for a mortgage.
- Have them read your home buying guide. Say you will discuss it in detail at your next meeting.
- Have them fill out a questionnaire on their home buying criteria.

For sellers, here are some tasks or assignments to qualify their commitment:

- Ask them to contact their lender to get an updated accounting of their payoff amount.
- Ask them to do a pre-home inspection on their house.
- Request that they clean out their house, remove clutter or otherwise begin preparations to show their house before your next meeting.

It's not important what you ask them to do, but whether or not they do it. If they don't follow up, you have to seriously consider how interested and qualified they are.

I want to discuss the "fit" between real estate agent and client a little bit more. I think it's important for us as real estate agents to always work with clients who want to work with us, and who we are motivated to work with. If the client does not respect and value what you bring to the table as a real estate agent, your working relationship will not be as effective. By the same token, there are demands on our time as real estate agents. We should also be choosy about who we do business with.

An example of making sure you are working with clients who "fit" is whether or not a prospective client is willing to take direction from you. Let's say you get a floor call. The person on the phone wants you to show him a specific house in a neighboring city. He also asks you if you can show him other houses that are similar. You say you can, and you ask him to meet at your office beforehand so you can discuss his needs first. He says he can't do that. He just wants you to meet him at the house he's interested in seeing, and says he can go from there. Now what do you do? Do you think this will be a good fit? My instincts tell me it won't be. This prospective client is not willing to let you lead him through the process that is in your professional opinion best for him, which is not a good sign. As a professional real estate agent, you are in charge of the real estate purchase or sales process. When your clients work with you, they are buying the idea that your expertise and professional opinion is what they need to make the purchase or sale of their home happen.

Another example, let's say you are referred a seller who wants to list their house, but the house is located about 45 minutes away from your office. This is a tough decision. You are busy. Can you provide the level of service and attention to this listing that is needed? If you take it, will any of your other clients suffer? The issue I would consider is the amount of time required to meet the seller's expectations. If I think this far-away seller will require more time than I can afford to pull away from my other clients, I will refer the seller to another real estate agent. I would take the time to pre-screen this real estate agent, because even in this referral my professional reputation is on the line.

You should remove the word "please" from all of your communications with potential clients. Its use is a pet peeve of mine, because begging is not selling. I believe that if you start out saying "please work with me," you are putting yourself in a weak position. Your future clients, even the ones you have not worked with yet, need to see your value without you having to say "please." Make sure you don't use the word please in your marketing collateral, in your initial meetings with prospective clients, or anywhere on your website. Just use positive action statements. No matter how thin your pipeline is, you never have to beg.

Opportunity Costs: What Are They for Real Estate Agents?
The economic cost of using a resource for a specific activity is equal to the income foregone by not using it for an alternative activity. You're saying, "Whoa, this is a sales book not an economics class!" But this concept, also known as "opportunity cost," is extremely important for you to understand. For real estate agents, the

"resource" is your time. Once you spend time with a client, that time is gone. You will never get it back, and you cannot use it for any other sales activity.

So consider how challenging a prospective client's needs are to meet. Always be aware that the time you spend with this prospective client will not be available to use with another, better-qualified client. This is a risk, and in the end it could cost you money.

How much will it cost you? Say, for example, you decide to work with a challenging client based on her criteria and budget. You decide to go for it, because the commission payout is $12,000 for the type of house she wants. You spend time with her, and after five tours you show her 30 houses. You write a contract on a house she kind of likes, but isn't 100 percent thrilled about. It's a low-ball offer, and does not result in a contract. You then go out and view another 20 homes over three more tours with her. At the end of the day, the client says she isn't seeing what she wants. She tells you she wants to wait until next summer.

"Okay," you think to yourself, "this is sales, these things happen, and as a result, I've lost out on $12,000 commission. Bummer!" Bad news though: we have still not calculated your total loss on this client. You were also talking to another buyer, and your qualifying questions told you he was kind of lukewarm. You lost touch with him when you got busy with your challenging buyer. You find out this second buyer went to a new construction development, loved what he saw, and bought a house out of their inventory which would have been an $8,000 commission for you. So the true opportunity cost of your decision to work with the first buyer is $20,000.

This is why it is so important for you to qualify prospects well and spend your time wisely. If you have been a real estate agent for more than five years, you have probably been in a situation or two similar to this. I know I have, especially in my busier spring and summer seasons. It's impossible to close every client we work with, so understanding opportunity cost is crucial.

In summary, it's very important to spend your time wisely with well-qualified clients. They should be a good fit for you, and fit the profile for making a decision. This will ensure getting under contract and making it to more successful closings.

Do You Suffer From Call Reluctance?
There is a chronic condition among salespeople called "call reluctance." Any of us can fall into this trap, and it can have very negative consequences. Here's how the scenario plays out. A web inquiry comes into your email Inbox. A prospective client requests that a real estate agent please call to discuss a house she saw for sale in her neighborhood. You get the email in the morning, but you decide it's probably best not to call right away, so you plan to call in the afternoon. Later that day you

get really busy with a client. At 5pm you see the web inquiry email again and say to yourself, "I shouldn't call so late in the day; I'll call first thing in the morning."

Here's another example of call reluctance. You are going to hold an open house this coming Sunday. Your plan is to call some of your past clients on Wednesday who might be interested in stopping by on Sunday. You put together a list on Tuesday so you have it ready for your Wednesday morning calls. When you get to work on Wednesday, the first thing you decide to do is clean out your desk a bit, archive some of your older files, and go through your entire Inbox to make sure that there are no outstanding issues. You find some internal office paperwork issues for a closing you have coming up in two weeks that you simply must address. All of a sudden you look up and realize it's already lunch time and the morning has gotten away from you. The phone calls you had planned on doing get pushed to another day.

Finally, you get a referral from a past client via email. Your past client says to call right away because their friend is actively looking for a real estate agent, and includes their friend's contact information. What a great lead! You decide it's a good time to go through your entire email Inbox to make sure there are no other great leads out there that you are neglecting. After about a half hour, you decide it's time for lunch and that you'd rather make the call on a full stomach.

I think you get the idea of where I'm going with these examples. All of us, in some form or another have had a case of call reluctance. It's just part of being in sales. It's a dirty little secret we don't talk about. Often, salespeople will not even accept that they have a problem until their entire pipeline has dried up. Having the discipline to make your calls ensures your success as a real estate agent because it keeps the top of your sales pipeline full. As I mentioned before, I've been in sales all of my professional life so I have seen both mild and extreme cases of call reluctance. The good news is, if you have this problem, you are not alone. There are ways to solve it, and in the next few minutes I'll show you how.

At my first sales job, I worked in a phone room where a group of us were making phone calls out of the phone book directly to people in their homes. This was tough selling, but I was young. Our managers made a game out of it, and motivated us to compete with each other based on how many contacts and sales we made. We would pound the phone and make on average 80-100 dials in a four hour period. Needless to say, I didn't last long in this job and was only there for about 6 months. It was just brutal getting rejected so many times, and it wore me down.

My next job, my first after graduating from college, was as a computer software sales rep. Again I had to make cold calls, but this time it was to businesses, which was better than calling people at home at random out of the phone book. I had the experience and thick skin from making the calls so it was easy for me to do.

I got lucky, because during this job I came across the book, the *One Minute Sales Person* which I have already mentioned. The psychological shift my mind took after reading this book enabled me to be an even better phone prospector because I was now "selling on purpose." This book taught me that I had a product of value that would benefit the businesses I was calling, which removed any remaining anxiety about making the calls. This mental shift led me to a successful sales career in high tech, and then in real estate.

As a real estate agent, it is very easy for me to justify every call or meeting with a prospective client because I am confident that I offer real value. I know I can help my client accomplish their goal to buy or sell their home, which eliminates any reluctance to make the call that will start this process for them. You too can overcome any call reluctance or sales anxiety you have if you truly believe in the unique value you can bring to your clients.

Inertia is also an impediment to making your calls or scheduling that meeting. A trick that works well for me is to make an easier call first to get warmed up. Make that follow up phone call or feedback call first and then immediately make your important call. Just get into motion and you won't think twice before making your call or having your meeting.

The next time you are agonizing over making phone calls or meeting clients for the first time, remind yourself of how effective you are at helping your clients, and that you are good at what you do. As real estate agents, we often work alone with little support or praise. Sometimes when I get worn down I will go back and read my client testimonials. These kind words are important to keep on hand as a marketing tool, but also for many other reasons. Besides being a great ego boost, they put me in a good mood and remind me of why I got into real estate in the first place, and that I am good at what I do. When I go into a call or meeting with good feelings and confidence about what I do, I can't help but be successful.

Develop Good Work Habits
Discipline and good work habits are so important for real estate agents. If you don't develop a good work routine, you will develop bad habits that are hard to break. Good work habits keep you on track and working towards your goals. Bad habits will put you out of business. Everyone knows this, so why bring it up? It is easy for us as real estate agents to slack off, because we do not have a manager watching our every move and keeping track of our sales activities. Most individual real estate agents who work for large companies are on their own when it comes to their work schedule and daily routine. In my opinion, the lack of a structured work environment is one of the key reasons that many real estate agents end up not being successful.

Did you go into real estate because you wanted to be your own boss, or because you don't enjoy working for people? If so, you may be disappointed. We all work for someone or something, even if this "boss" becomes the income you either make or don't make. When you have your own business you have to do everything you can to generate an income so you can pay your bills and stay in business. If you goof off or play hooky when you work for yourself, you won't be in business long because no money will be coming in. Real estate agents who are not able to develop good work habits and a business process will be out of real estate in six months or less.

How do you maintain a good work schedule? Discipline and focus are the keys. As real estate agents, when business is good we can get busy very quickly. This means it is important to stick to a work routine during the week to make time for our calls, our appointments, our office time, and our personal or family time. During the busy times when we have multiple clients and deals going on at the same time, it can be easier to prioritize. When things slow down for us, it is even more critical to stay focused and on top of our game. Don't procrastinate and do what is fun, do what is important. Do the things that will make you successful. Woody Allen, comedian and filmmaker, may have said it best when he said that "80% of success is showing up." You need to figure this out this for yourself. I can't tell you what type of work schedule to maintain, but it needs to be one that works for you and it needs to be consistent.

For example, some people can work from home while others can't. If you can't focus and do your work at home, then you need to get into the office every morning. At times, I have been able to work from home. But if my kids are around, experience has shown me that I will get nothing accomplished. My daughters will hijack my computer, and we end up watching YouTube videos of their favorite songs. So even on the weekends I go into the office if I need to complete a task.

Setting a routine can be difficult for real estate agents because we often work when other people are off. When we are busy, this can mean working seven days a week. We have appointments in the evenings and we work on the weekends. I remember when I first started working as a real estate agent how hard it was for me to work on Saturdays and Sundays. Since college, I had jobs where I only worked during the week. I never had to disrupt my weekend with a client meeting. Initially, it was a shock to my system to work on the weekends, but over time I got used to it. Now I don't even think about it because it helps me serve my clients more effectively, and it helps me close deals. It is beneficial to my business and personal success as a real estate agent, so I happily do it. Plus, I don't get the "Sunday Night Blues" anymore.

Good Work Habits Help You Accomplish Your Personal Goals
Whenever I think of "focus", I think of "goals". Why are you working? What is pulling you to the future? What is driving you? What is important to you? We all know the

truly successful people and high earners are the ones who are focused and driven. Here is a good exercise for you to do as you think about your daily routine. Pull out a blank sheet of paper or open a blank Word document and write on the top: "What is important to me?" Take a deep breath and think. There are a lot of goal setting exercises out there, but to me it all boils down to this fundamental question. Write down what is important to you, not what others expect of you, or what you think you should write. Write what is in your heart. You will find that the things that are important to you are often different than what family and friends expect of you. Having a goal or multiple goals that you define for yourself is what will keep you going and pull you to the future. A goal will keep you focused on the work and activities you need to do every day.

When I was growing up, I remember watching an episode from the TV show *Taxi*, called "The Art of Cab Driving." The episode is brilliant satire and you should watch it if you can. It's funny and entertaining, but paints a vivid picture of how valuable it is to have a goal. At the beginning of the episode, Jim Ignatowski is the worst cab driver of the group. Part of his route that day involves picking up a couple of businessmen at the airport. Jim overhears their discussion about a new secret to success called "dynamic perfectionism" and ends up attending a life-changing seminar on the topic.

The episode is both poking fun at these types of self-improvement seminars, and making an important point about goal setting. When he gets back, Jim is so excited about what he has learned that he tells the rest of the cab drivers how important it is to have a goal, something that we want more than anything else in this world. He explains that if you do every little thing in your life the best you can, and do it perfectly, you will attain your goal. Jim had a goal that was only important to him, but by the end of the show he had accomplished it and was recognized as the best cab driver in the group.

Chapter 15

Congratulations! You are a Marketing Executive!

It's great to have all of these newfound skills as a real estate agent, but nothing happens until you find some people who decide to use your services. You have two primary job responsibilities as a real estate agent. One is to service your clients by helping them sell or buy their property. The other is to communicate to the public that you are a real estate agent, so they know of your services and then choose you to be their agent. Sounds pretty simple, right? Service and marketing: that's it when you boil it down. Focus on what is important and only do activities related to these two job functions.

You can be the greatest real estate agent in the world, providing the best service out there, and still be out of business within a year if no one knows about you. You have to get the word out that you are a real estate agent. You have to promote the expertise, value, and unique perspective you bring to the marketplace, and the niche you have chosen to specialize in.

Let's take a closer look at marketing today for real estate agents. You are marketing yourself as the product. If you market yourself correctly, clients will come to you and choose you to be their real estate agent based on your expertise.

If you are a real estate agent, does it make sense to say, "stop selling houses" since you sell houses for a living? My premise is that to be successful as a real estate agent today and in the future, you need to sell and market *yourself* as the product, rather than focusing on just selling houses. Your success long term is based on the strong relationships you build with your clients. The snowball effect of repeat business and referrals is the equity you are building in yourself and in your business.

Customers will choose to work with you based on these three factors:

1. Your expertise and knowledge in your area of specialization.

2. How you market and promote yourself to potential clients, past clients, and your sphere of contacts. Are you building relationships with new clients? Are you maintaining strong relationships with past clients?

3. The value of your service as perceived by your clients when they choose you to be their real estate agent.

Once you get your real estate license and start working, you are going to be a target for a ton of companies and people who are going to try and sell you all kinds of things. Initially, you will have to buy business cards and "for sale" signs at a minimum. And depending on who you work for, you might not even have to buy these.

Remember what I said before; you want to set yourself apart from your competition. Times have changed, and the old-school marketing methods are just not as effective anymore. Potential clients will want to work with you based on the value they perceive you offer them, not because you sent them a generic newsletter or a refrigerator magnet.

Here's a quick outline for a marketing plan for your first year, including associated costs. I will go through each of these in more detail in the coming chapters.

- Create a Facebook fan page for yourself—FREE

- Get on LinkedIn and create a profile. Start connecting with friends, past colleagues and other contacts you know—FREE

- Set up a Twitter account and start tweeting—FREE

- Create and set up a blog on ActiveRain or WordPress. There is a fee to be what they call a "Rainmaker" on ActiveRain, which gives you the features and capabilities you need. In 2010, my one-year fee for ActiveRain was $349. WordPress blogs are free (as of this writing).

- Post videos of yourself on YouTube discussing meaningful and relevant information on your niche market—FREE

- Your company web page should have a spot to plug in a profile page about you—this should be FREE

- Mailers are a good idea only if you have a geographic niche or "farm", as some people call it. This is the part of a marketing budget where you could spend a lot of money. To give you an idea, when I mail out 225 color, jumbo post cards, it costs me around $170 including first class postage.

- Personalized networking by you with your sphere of contacts—FREE

- Traditional Marketing Methods—spend no more than $200 to $300 in this area at the most in your first year.

Your goal for your first year as a real estate agent is to spend no money or *as little money as possible on marketing yourself.* Believe me, you are going to be bombarded by so many different companies promising you that their products or services will increase your sales and generate leads for you. Don't listen to them; it's a complete waste of time! Do not spend the money in your first year to build and create your own personalized web page, and DO NOT buy one of the generic, boiler plate websites for your own web page.

There *are* some traditional marketing methods which might still work for you, and the 21st Century Marketing tactics I have mentioned above are quite effective. You *can* get the word out very effectively these days for little to no money. In the coming chapters I will show you how.

Chapter 16
21st Century Marketing

Social media is all the rage nowadays. If you don't have a Facebook account then you're not cool! Are you tweeting yet? How many people have you connected with on LinkedIn? What about blogging? Are you tearing up the blogosphere with your knowledge? And as time goes by, there are going to be more and more social media content sites for us to use personally and for our businesses. Today and heading into the future you will have to be in tune with social media, especially if you are new and building your personal brand and identity in the marketplace.

Be careful about using social media as an excuse to not work. A popular term lately is "Social Not Working." I just say this because you might get distracted and spend too much time on social media.

I want to also caution you: Social media should not be your only marketing effort; it is just one tool to use in your marketing tool kit as a real estate agent. Social media is a way to connect and maintain relationships with your sphere and potential new customers.

Before I go into a discussion of some of the relevant social media programs, I'd like to give you my five tips for being effective on social media.

Top 5 Tips for Social Media

1. Be Authentic, Be Genuine

2. Care about what you do—what is your motivation? Help your clients—how you feel comes through in your messaging.

3. Create valuable content for your target audience.

4. Bill Gates once said, "content is king"—for real estate agents I say, "video is king."

5. Don't Sell—Don't Push

Let's go through each of the social media platforms that are useful for real estate agents:

Facebook

Facebook has over 950 million users as of this writing in 2012. It connects people of all ages from all over world. Recent world events have demonstrated the power of Facebook. (Egypt / Tunisia / Jordan / Yemen revolutions)

My father, who is over 70 years old, is a big Facebook user. As of this writing he has just over 1,000 friends from all over the world. And to think, just ten years ago my father was not even using email on his computer! In the past few years the largest group of people who started using Facebook were those aged 65 and older. It helps them stay in touch with family and friends, view pictures and videos, and feel connected even when they are at home alone.

The reason I use my father as an example is that I know many real estate agents who are completely resisting using Facebook. I don't understand the resistance myself. If my father can use Facebook, then anyone can; there is no excuse.

How can Facebook work for you as a real estate agent? Here are two ways to get started:

1) Create a "fan" page for yourself or your business entity, OR
2) Use your personal account to keep in touch with friends and business contacts.

Here are the pros and cons of these different methods of promoting yourself as a real estate agent on Facebook:

1) If you choose to use a "fan" page, you can post information related to your niche and local market there. "Fan" pages are definitely more business-oriented than personal pages. I would say most Facebook users who "fan" a person or business entity would not be surprised to receive marketing information as a result. You can then link your blog posts to your Facebook "fan" page and have it post automatically or periodically. You can also manually link the blog yourself based on whether or not you feel it's appropriate.

2. Another option is to use your personal Facebook account the usual way, to stay in touch with friends, family, and past clients. If you go this route, I suggest you try *not* to be overly sales-oriented on your personal page. Every now and then you can post real estate related information, but make sure not to go overboard. Just be yourself; otherwise you might be "de-friended" by some of the people you want to stay in touch with.

Regardless of the option you choose, be sure to post lots of pictures, videos and links on Facebook that you think will catch the interest of your prospective and current clients. I have been blown away by the quality and ease of posting and sharing videos on Facebook. You can also attach links, including news articles, web pages, and other items you think will be of interest to your Facebook "fans" or friends. Relevant pictures, videos, and links are all excellent ways to keep people informed of your niche and local market.

LinkedIn

LinkedIn is also a great site for professional networking. As Facebook, there is no charge to get signed up; all you need to do is create and build your profile. Think of your LinkedIn profile as a resume, and build it in a way so that prospective clients will be impressed. Highlight your areas of expertise, years of experience, niche, and accomplishments. Be sure to include any awards you have won in previous jobs and currently as a real estate agent. Once you build your profile, start working on building your network by connecting with people in your sphere. LinkedIn makes it very easy to import all of your email contacts and send out invitations for people to connect with you.

Next, join some Groups on LinkedIn, such as your college alumni or networking group, area or regional groups, groups that have to do with your niche or area of expertise, and trade or professional groups. Once you join some groups, you can start learning more about the people in the group and their interests and start networking with them.

The most important thing to do on LinkedIn is to connect with your past clients. Send them a request for a recommendation, LinkedIn's version of a testimonial. Try to get as many recommendations on your profile as possible. Recommendations on LinkedIn will give you great credibility with prospective clients.

Stick with it. LinkedIn is very user-friendly, can be enjoyable, and doesn't require a huge time commitment. But to be successful with any of these social networking tools, you need to stay active. Be sure to log in, check your messages, and respond to requests in a timely manner to build your brand and make your presence known.

Twitter

Twitter is a good fit for Realtors, especially when you "tweet" about your niche or chosen area of expertise. In time, you will develop followers who care about what you have to say. Twitter can be a great way to get the word out about an open house, new listing, or recent success, but make sure these aren't the only things you "tweet" about. Focus less on selling and transactions, and more on valuable information about your geographic area or niche that your followers will find useful. If you are selective about whom you "follow," you can keep things more professional on Twitter and eliminate a lot of "noise" and distractions. To be successful on Twitter definitely requires you to be purposeful, and to keep up a regular schedule of quality tweets to develop the type of following you want.

Realtor Blogs

Blogging is very important and an excellent way to get your content on the Internet. The easiest way to start is to join ActiveRain, a blogging site specifically for real estate agents and real estate. There is a fee involved to be a "Rainmaker" and have the functionality you need, as I mentioned in my section on your first year marketing plan and costs.

But, if you take a little more time and effort, I highly recommend setting up a blog on WordPress. The reason I say this is that WordPress is very Google-friendly in terms of searches on Google. WordPress blogs are great for mobile devices because they format your blog properly on mobile devices such as tablets and smartphones. The other nice aspect of WordPress is that it's free.

Blogging requires an even bigger time commitment than keeping up with the social networking sites. You need to have a commitment to writing, something valuable to say, and you should be adding content on a regular basis to give your audience something to look forward to, so they keep coming back to read more. Writing a blog and keeping it up is a lot of work, but it can be very valuable in building your niche, and can really highlight your expertise as a Realtor.

I bet you are saying, "this sounds good, but what do I blog about?" Relevant and meaningful information! Just as with the other social networking you do, you want to make sure you add value to your potential clients. On ActiveRain for example, you can learn from other agents. How do they blog? What information looks interesting to you? You can't blog too much, so don't worry about posting a lot of information.

When I blog, I post information focused on my geographic area for people who are considering a move to the area. That is my niche and it works well for me. I also let my personality and who I am shine through in my blog posts. Post pictures! They break up the text and make your blog more interesting and readable. Keep your posts short and sweet. Consider breaking up that one long blog post idea into three smaller posts, or a "blog series."

YouTube Videos

Online videos accomplish two objectives for you: they demonstrate your expertise and value as a Realtor, and they give people an opportunity to connect with you at a very personal level. I started using YouTube to target prospective clients, and to my surprise I found out a lot of my past clients and people from my sphere were also watching and forwarding my videos to each other. I received a lot of positive feedback; everyone was so enthusiastic and told me how much they enjoyed watching them. Remember, the relationship you have with your clients is very important. Videos are an excellent and very personal way to establish or reestablish a relationship.

I know you are asking yourself, "Is this guy serious? Do I really have to do real estate agent videos? I can't do that! How will I look? I need to lose some weight. How will my hair look? I will be way too nervous!" As I mentioned in a previous chapter, I was a little reluctant at first myself, but now that I've done a few of them, I can't wait to do more. You just have to get over that initial hurdle in your mind and go for it. Once you do your first video, you will get over all of these objections because the payoff is worth it.

Doing a video is no different than any other presentation you have done before, and in today's competitive market, this is a way to set yourself apart from your competition. Just be yourself and imagine you are talking to a client who is really going to benefit from what you have to say. You have many types of content to choose from for a video, so get creative and think about what people in your niche and past clients would want to see a presentation about. Remember not to make this a hard-core sales presentation or you risk coming across as just another salesperson. Put some time in, research your topic, and put together a valuable presentation for your target market. Make sure you say you are the expert in the niche you discuss! This is where you get to shine, be an expert, and provide something of value to your sphere.

Think of yourself as a movie star! Videos are a great way to be more visible on the web. Post them on YouTube, and before you know it you will start getting views. In time, you'll start getting leads from the videos—I did!

Your Own Personalized Web Page
Finally, make sure you have a personalized web page. If your company gives you a profile page on their site, make sure to take advantage of this. Get a good picture, post a brief bio about yourself, and start adding testimonials from past clients. In the first couple of years it's not necessary to spend a lot of money on a fancy personalized web page, unless you have the skills and resources to do so yourself, or know someone who can do it for you at a good price. I know agents who have spent up to $10,000 on a web page; the trouble is, sometimes it works and sometimes it doesn't. In your first year, it's not a good use of your time to be an IT Executive in addition to all of your other responsibilities. If you feel strongly about having your own page and distinct URL, then I recommend starting out with a one page web site highlighting yourself, your niche, and some testimonials. I will discuss this more in the next chapter concerning your personal website.

The Bottom Line
To be successful as a real estate agent today, you not only have to accept social media, you have to really embrace it and focus on building a presence online. I believe you cannot be successful without it, especially if you are just starting out. I have met a lot of agents through social media, and some of them are senior to me in age and years of experience in real estate. I imagine many of these agents did not grow up using computers, much less the Internet. Yet some of these older

agents are doing a great job online promoting themselves, writing excellent blogs, and letting their personality shine through on the web. Unfortunately I know a lot of agents who are resisting the new world of social media. I see their sales results suffer because of their inability to adapt and change with the times we live in.

Get used to change in social media! The more adaptable and flexible you are, the better you'll do. A couple of years ago I was a LinkedIn power user and not as active on Facebook. Today my feelings are reversed. I have really come to value the interactive, personal nature of Facebook. Real estate is a very personal business, and I don't mind letting clients into my life a little by being myself on Facebook. Each year there are new social media programs popping up—this past year we saw the rise of Google Plus and Pinterest. Who knows? In a few years there will be other popular social networking sites that we all will be using.

The old *Field of Dreams* adage, "when you build it, they will come," applies here. When you create a presence online, clients will find you based on your specialty and the expertise you offer. As Bill Gates said in 1996, "content is king." I personally have been building quality content online over the years by blogging, posting YouTube videos, and updating my web page in a personalized way. I continue to get well-qualified leads as a result of these efforts. The clients who find me online and call me have already decided to use my services as a real estate agent, because they have already developed a relationship with me. The following are some of the comments I hear when they call for the first time:

- "I just watched you on YouTube."
- "I see you specialize in relocation."
- "I saw all of your customer testimonials on your web page."
- "I looked at all the pictures you have online in Boulder."
- "I see you live in Louisville and that's where I want to live."

The meaningful content I have built online is found by the clients who fit my business model. It is then an obvious choice when they choose me to be their real estate agent. The content I have built is also beneficial for referrals. I am finding that many of my referred clients view my content online, get a comfort level with me, and then call or email.

Some real estate agents are intimidated by the Internet, but I've found it to be a beautiful thing. My content is always there, and as long as I keep updating it, my prospective clients will find me. Your clients will find you too, once you put this chapter's advice into action. Have faith, keep blogging, posting videos on YouTube, and staying in touch with your sphere via social media and you too will see results.

Chapter 17
Personal Website: The Foundation of Your Brand

One of the things that amazes me every day is how many real estate agents do not have their own personal website with their own URL. So many agents just use the boilerplate provided by their office, or a prepackaged template they pay for. These are typically unattractive, framed-in websites that are not personalized at all. Often they contain just the agent's picture and contact information. Most real estate companies have their own website that includes pages for all of their agents. Sometimes they will provide you with your own one page bio, but is that enough to be competitive today? As with any business, it is crucial today to have your own website which you manage and where all the leads and inquiries go directly to you. Think of your website as your store front in retail terms. If you don't have a store, how are people going to do business with you?

What do you want to achieve with your website? Here are the goals you should set out to accomplish:

- Use quality content to present yourself as a real estate agent with expertise in your chosen niche or area of focus.
- Start developing a relationship with your prospective client through a highly personalized website.
- Generate leads and inquiries in the form of emails or phone calls from people who come to your website.

Done correctly, your website will present you, in a personal way, as an expert. This builds credibility and trust, and prospective clients will want you to be their real estate agent. A strong website is also important for referrals. Let's say a prospective client gets your name from one of your past clients and they don't know much about you. These days they are most likely to go right to their computer, run a search for your name, and check out your website. If you are presented well online, it will begin to sell the prospective client on your services before you even have your first conversation.

Now that you have chosen your niche, you can build your website around your area of expertise. Content and personalization are key. Your content will help prospective clients both find you and become interested in you. Over time, you should keep adding niche-oriented, up-to-date content that is of value to your prospective clients. This is going to require a lot of work on your end, but it will pay off if you do it right.

A quick word about website addresses: Many agents use their name as their website address. The problem with this is that your name has no meaning to prospective clients, and they will not remember it. Ideally, you should choose a website address or URL that is tied to your niche. For example, if you are specializing in horse properties, get a URL such as www.horseproperties(your city).com. Or, if you are doing vacation properties you can use some variation of www.vacationhomes(city).com. Choose an easy-to-remember website address that further ties into your niche, and you will see your business grow.

Real estate agents are relationship salespeople, so your website should be structured to sell you as a person and an individual. As soon as prospects hit your website they will start to develop a relationship with you and either identify with you immediately or not. Personalize your website so people will feel as if they know you and want to work with you. Put yourself out there. Include good pictures of yourself, client testimonials, and relevant videos of you.

Collecting testimonials from your numerous happy clients is especially important. Take a picture of your clients at the "walk-through" before the closing, and ask them if you can include it next to their testimonial on your website. Your clients will be delighted to help you out in this way, and this makes a great impression on prospective customers who visit your page. Testimonials speak directly to what makes your services unique, so include multiple testimonials, and give your prospects a compelling reason to get in touch with you. If you don't, they will move on to another website and you will lose out on their business. Remember that you are the product, and testimonials are one of the strongest ways to sell yourself to prospective clients.

You also need to include videos of you discussing issues pertinent to your area of expertise on your website. The videos should add value to your prospects by being interesting and educational but **not** blatantly sales-oriented. This way, your prospective clients see you in person, start building a relationship with you right there online, and get the sense that you understand their specific needs. You might be saying, "There is no way I am doing a video!" I felt that way too, but once I started doing videos for my customers and prospects, I realized what a strong selling tool it was for me. Just sit down in front of a camera, visualize yourself talking to one of your customers, and it will come naturally to you.

It is not necessary to fill your website with property listings. Your website is designed to sell you as a real estate agent, so having listings or an Internet Data Exchange (IDX) search for listings is not really important, and can be distracting. When people search for homes online these days, they have many options, including Realtor.com, Remax.com, Zillow.com, Trulia.com, and hundreds more. You're not in the business of competing with these huge sites, nor do you have to. It's okay to have some niche-oriented listings and your own listings on the site, but it's not necessary to have an IDX. They are costly and not worth it for your purposes. Internet traffic studies show that people do search the Internet to find a real estate agent after they find listings of interest on these sites. This is where your personal website comes in and will pay off for you.

The way to generate more leads for your business today is with valuable, up-to-date content, and an online presence that sells you, the real estate agent, as the product. When you have an area of expertise that clients want, they will find you quickly on the web rather than you having to find them. You can still prospect via a database of names, and use mailers, phone calls, and hand-written notes, but these techniques will not sustain you on their own. Without a presence on the web, your business will not grow.

The type of website I am talking about is not cheap. The biggest percentage of your marketing budget has to go into your website. This is a must, and I can't stress its importance enough. Once you build your website focused on your specialty, you will start getting leads based on your niche. These leads will be a much better "fit" for you, because they are drawn to the specific knowledge and expertise you have built your website around. They are pre-qualified prospective buyers and sellers, and they want to work with you.

Here's a good analogy: Would you rather have a floor call lead with a buyer who wants to see a listing, or a buyer referred from a previous customer of yours? If the price ranges were the same, which would you choose? Of course you would choose the referral. It's a much hotter lead since your previous customer has "pre-sold" you to them. A floor lead does not care who you are, they just want to see the house. You don't even know if they are qualified or ready to buy now. A web lead from your website built around your niche is a very warm lead similar to a referral lead.

How do I create this Awesome Website?
The big question here is, "Who do I get to do my niche-based website?" This is a difficult question since most of us are not computer experts. We have to trust someone else to do this for us, and it is a leap of faith most times. A good strategy is to view some other websites (not necessarily agent websites) to see what catches your eye.

Here's a checklist of questions for you to answer before you partner with a website developer or Internet marketing company.

1. What websites do you find appealing?
2. How do you want to be involved in the process short and long term? How much effort are you willing to put in?
3. Who is your target audience? What type of homes are your targets looking for in terms of price and location?
4. What are your strengths and weaknesses as a real estate agent?
5. What is your budget to get the website launched initially, and what is your budget for ongoing website maintenance?
6. What are your goals for your website?
7. How will people find your website?
8. Is there any specific technology you want developed? For example, do you want your listings included on your site? Do you want those listings to be searchable?
9. What type of content do you want on the website?
10. How often will you be updating your content?
11. What are you currently doing to market yourself?
12. Do you have existing marketing collateral? Is it effective?
13. Do you have an existing website? What do and don't you like about it?
14. What questions do you have in general about the Internet as a marketing tool, and specifically about the process of creating your website?

To create and manage a website requires you to partner with a website developer and marketer, a company with experience creating websites that generate results for their clients. Your website developer and marketer also must be well versed in Search Engine Optimization (SEO). Today, it's not enough to create a good website that contains your company information. People are searching for real estate information online all the time, and more real estate agents than ever have an online presence. This means you have to get the most qualified prospects for your market niche to your page via the search engines.

I have been working with MarketiQ, an Internet marketing consulting company. We have developed a strong partnership in creating and maintaining my website. I was lucky because I found a company that understood my business. We collaborate and brainstorm on ideas to help make my website a better experience for my prospective clients.

I recommend you create a website unique to you. There are a lot of companies out there who sell pre-packaged template-driven websites for agents. But why would you want to have the website that everyone else has? It just does not make sense to me. Creating your own site from scratch will cost more money than the cookie cutter websites, but it's worth the investment. It will generate real, qualified leads for you over time, which will translate into closings.

Over the long run, your website will generate more commissions for you. Let's use some easy numbers as an example. Let's say today you are averaging around ten closings a year, and this business is coming mainly from the following four sources: your referrals from past clients, repeat business, business created from your listings, and general networking. For this example, you are currently not receiving web leads of any kind that are translating into closings. You then create the niche-oriented website I have discussed, and in the second year after the site is up, you get two additional closings originating from your website. The third year you close three of these web leads, and the fourth year you close four. Since you are still averaging around ten closings per year based on other lead sources, by year two you have already grown your business by twenty percent. You have added more qualified customers to your pipeline, and you will make more income. The math won't work out this way exactly, but I am using this example to show how much an effective, personalized website can add to your existing business. This adds to your referral and repeat business and creates a snowball effect, a good thing for a real estate agent seeking a long and successful career.

Chapter 18
Traditional Marketing Methods

I personally do not believe in, nor engage in, most of the old school marketing methods for real estate agents. Still, this chapter is necessary, because I know that some of them still work for other real estate agents. Some might work for you based on your local market and niche. I'll go through them briefly so you can determine whether or not they apply to you.

Knocking on Doors: A number of agents go door-to-door, canvassing a neighborhood when they get a new listing in that neighborhood. The approach is, "I just listed a house in your neighborhood. I wanted to share the sales price with you to see if you know of anyone who might be interested in moving here." Homeowners are pretty universally interested in the going price for homes in their neighborhood, since this affects their personal investment in their own home. They are also almost invariably interested in having "good neighbors," so the idea of referring someone they know will also be appealing. But the true intent is not necessarily to find a prospective buyer for your listing house, but rather to start a conversation, build a relationship, and add this prospective client to your sphere for follow up. When they are ready to sell their house you can help them and get the listing.

Phone Prospecting: Some agents call potential clients every day, others make it a point to call their sphere at least once a month. Cold calling out of the phone book on other potential clients is another strategy many real estate agents employ. Personally, given all of the other communication tools we have, I feel phone prospecting is just outdated. Cold calling people at home is more frowned upon than ever, there are "Do Not Call" lists to comply with, and this tactic is definitely not going to win you any popularity contests.

This is not to be confused, however, with picking up the phone to call your "warm" or "hot" leads, including giving a call to respond to a web or email inquiry, letting prospects know about an open house they might be interested in, or following up with a referral. This must be done religiously.

Host Open Houses: This is a good method, especially when you're new, to get yourself out there and meet people. I did this quite a bit in my early years. I had a colleague who was a big "lister," and she was kind enough to let me hold open houses for some of her listings. I learned a lot meeting people face-to-face, both people from the neighborhood where the listing was, and people who were interested in the house. Pursue teaming up with another agent representing the seller to host his or her open house if you don't have any listings yet. I was able to convert a good number of open house attendees into clients, who I subsequently helped buy a house.

Goodies at the Door: If your niche is a geographic neighborhood, you might consider canvassing the neighborhood with a "gift" of some kind. Agents often leave items such as these at the front door, along with marketing materials and a business card. This is where you can get creative and do something different. Think of a gift that would be unique and interesting to the neighborhood, like a child's plastic beach bucket and sand shovel in a waterfront neighborhood. I have never done this, but I am sure you can come up with some creative ideas.

Leads Groups: I have participated in a few "leads groups." The idea is to get a group of 10-15 professionals in your area, each representing a specific business service or product segment, none in competition with the other. So for example, you might join a group that includes a doctor, a lawyer, a physical therapist, a childcare proprietor, and a landscape architect. The group then shares leads back and forth with each other. You don't sell your product or service to each other, but you do share your contacts.

Unfortunately, the leads groups I joined did not work for me. The attendees focused on selling their products and services to each other. I wanted to get access to their clients with joint marketing efforts but was not able to do so. I found them a waste of my time—and time is money to us as agents.

I do know someone who started his own leads group from the ground up. He was able to generate a number of good, quality leads which led to real business. If I were starting out, I would look at creating my own leads group. I feel my friend was successful because he had more credibility with the group and he was able to structure the format of the leads group in a way to help generate leads for himself.

Newspaper Advertising: I can't in good conscience recommend this anymore. It's costly and the return on investment is not worth it.

I have stopped print advertising completely and there are other Realtors I know who have done the same. I used to always do a newspaper ad to advertise an open house I was hosting on a weekend, but now I've found promoting the open house on the Internet via our MLS is much more effective.

Throwing good advertising money after print ads just doesn't make sense. It drains our budget and prevents us from putting our money into more effective advertising and marketing campaigns. The bottom line on print advertising is that, at best it will cost you money, and at worst it could put you out of business if you spend too much on it.

Sponsor a Community Event: Since you are new to real estate, I have already recommended you limit your marketing budget as much as possible. Sponsoring a community event could be an excellent strategy for you. I have seen agents sponsor and coordinate hiking trail cleanups, recycling drives, fundraising events for charities, children's sports teams, or senior food drives. The key here is to build your visibility locally within your community and show that you care and that you are involved.

Newsletters: Printed newsletters are out. I see a lot of agents today doing their newsletters online. These can be quite effective. Do some research, and find out from other agents you know whether there is a worthwhile and low-cost newsletter application you can use. Or simply create your own. Put together a good-looking, newsletter-style email and send it to your sphere. You can use content from your blog, but make sure it is timely, relevant, and helps your current and prospective clients get to know you and your niche better.

Mailers: There are good mailers and then there are terrible mailers. You have to be judicious in what you decide to send out to your target clients. If you have a geographic area you are farming, then a regular flow of mailers from you to your target audience can be effective. But, I caution you to make sure what you are sending is *of value to them*. Reports on the market and local issues, for example, would add value. Tell them something they don't already know!

I am not a fan of refrigerator magnets and junk mail and your target clients are not either. Maintain a level of professionalism in what you mail. Develop a consistent style so people will start identifying with you. If you get a new listing, send out postcards highlighting your new listing. When you close a deal, send out "Just Sold" postcards highlighting your successful sale with a picture of your customers on the postcard. Do not print the addresses on labels and then stick them on the cards. Get a mailing list to the postcard printer and have them print and mail the postcards for you. Pay whatever the additional cost is because this will save you time, and they will look clean and professional.

There are a lot of other traditional marketing methods that your peers, friends, colleagues, and salespeople trying to get you to buy their product will recommend. Take each one with a grain of salt. Before you commit to anything, weigh the cost and the return on your investment in terms of time and money. Please take into account how it will make you look to your sphere. People don't want a fly-by-night agent who is here one day, gone the next. They are looking for a levelheaded, professional real estate agent to help them with one of the most important purchasing decisions of their lives. You need to maintain a high level of professionalism in all marketing activities.

Chapter 19
Personal Networking

There's a fine line between selling to friends and family versus having friends and family help you. Done properly, you can have your friends and family help you in your career as a real estate agent. You want their help in getting the word out that you are now a real estate agent. You don't want them to feel as if you are selling to them specifically. It's like anything else; when you change a job or have anything new happen in your life, naturally you tell your friends and family. Now with social media this process is so much easier. In no time, you'll be able to get the word out about your new job as a real estate agent.

Promote your new job on Facebook and LinkedIn with all of your contacts. Be excited and share your enthusiasm for what you are doing now. Highlight the real estate niche you plan on specializing in so people know your plan. Your friends, family, and contacts will share your enthusiasm about your new job and some of them will be willing to help by referring potential clients to you.

Keep your sphere informed about how your career progresses by highlighting your successes along the way. Build a mailing list. I always mail out "Just Sold" postcards to my sphere, and I post updates via social media on my closings with a brief story of how the deal transpired. When I meet with people who are on my mailing list and who I am connected with on social websites, they always congratulate me on how well I am doing because they consistently hear my positive "Just Sold" news. A lot of them cheer me on and say, "another one for Mario!" or "Mario did it again!" It makes me feel good about what I do for a living when I know my sphere of contacts is supporting me and recognizing my successes. It's a great way to get the word out, plus it gives me an ego boost! We all need this from time to time, especially when we are in business for ourselves.

I believe there is an art to promoting yourself; do so in a positive way, without being too sales oriented. I post informational updates as well as my successes and steer clear of sales language. It just turns people off!

Here are some examples of language I feel is intrusive and way too sales oriented:

- "Now's a great time to buy."
- "Interest rates have never been lower than they are now."

- "Why it's better to buy than rent."
- "I am a top producer and the top agent in my office."
- "I just reached the million dollar mark and I can help you."
- "What is the value of your house? Call me today to find out."
- "Now's a great time to sell your house."

These types of postings online aggravate and irritate people. You don't want to alienate your sphere of contacts. The best referrals you get as a real estate agent come from past clients and people who know you. It's a people business and it's all about the strong relationships you build with your clients. By taking the honest approach all the time with your clients, you will set yourself apart from your competition.

When networking online and in person, always remember to have a level of humility and to have fun. People don't want to be around pompous gas bags; just be yourself. If you are inherently arrogant, tone it down a notch and it will help you.

There are a lot of good books about networking. Here are a few I suggest:

- ***Never Eat Alone*** by Keith Ferrazzi
- The classic ***How to Win Friends and Influence People*** by Dale Carnegie
- ***The Tipping Point*** by Malcolm Gladwell

When people know what you do for a living, you will find prospective clients wherever you go: the gym, local grocery store, library, restaurants, school functions for your kids, daycare, parks, and just about any public place. People will come to know what you do for a living eventually. Just weave it into your conversations in a natural way. "Really? That is good to know, because I am a Realtor." I drop this line on people so they know what I do for a living. The next time I see them, they know I am a real estate agent.

The next conversation you have with someone *will* (not *might*) turn into business. Always remember this when talking to people. The great thing about real estate is that everyone needs a roof over their head, so our universe of prospective customers is quite large. This is one of the reasons I got into the business! I think you will enjoy it as well.

Chapter 20
Money Is Time

No sales book is complete without a discussion on time management. Your most valuable asset is your time. How you choose to use your time will determine whether you succeed or fail as a real estate agent. No other factor has a bigger impact on your sales results and profitability as an agent. As you are starting out in your career in real estate, you will learn quickly which activities are profitable to you and which activities are a time drain and unprofitable.

You are your own business. Don't let anyone else tell you what you need to do with your time unless you are part of a team or a licensed assistant. The points I am making in this chapter are aimed at agents who are on their own and working as individual Realtors.

Your biggest challenge when starting out is that you don't know which activities are truly profitable and which activities are wastes of time. I know I wasted a lot of time in my early years with unqualified leads hoping that I could get a deal from them. In the end, and after a lot of wasted time, I discovered that these people were not qualified to either buy or sell. I wasted tons of time attending leads groups, Chamber of Commerce meetings, local trade shows, and all of my office meetings. Even I, a person with extensive sales experience, was sucked into these time wasting activities.

The daily, weekly, and monthly decisions you make concerning your time will determine your success more than any other factor, so you have to take time management seriously. Don't just go with the flow every day. Plan your days to use your time in the most productive way possible.

Ideally, you want to be either working on a marketing activity that is producing leads for you, or working on a sales situation with a client. Other times you will need to attend training classes to make sure you are current on your continuing education. Be careful not to get hooked on training classes and use this as an excuse to avoid the work which needs to be done daily. I have seen agents early in their career attend too many classes and seminars. They end up with minimal closings and then start complaining about the market and other issues. As a rule of thumb, I say no more than one to two-classes a month.

Have you seen the 1992 film *Glengarry Glen Ross*? It's a great movie based on a play by David Mamet about a Chicago real estate sales office. It has become a cult classic, especially among salespeople. The script can be shocking; it has a ton of profanity and it's very misogynistic, but very true to life. If you have worked in sales at all and are not easily offended, I think this movie will resonate with you.

"Coffee's for closers" is a well-known and often repeated monologue. It was not part of Mamet's original play, but written by Mamet specifically for Alec Baldwin and the movie. If you've seen it, you'll remember that Baldwin's character is sent by the owners of the real estate firm to improve the flagging efforts of their employees. His tactics include threats, intimidation, and a sales contest. One of my favorite lines from the script is "first prize is a Cadillac Eldorado, second prize, a set of steak knives, and third prize, you're fired." In a humiliating moment, one of the salespeople (played by Jack Lemmon in the movie) gets up to refill his coffee mug. "Coffee's for closers," says Baldwin, implying Lemmon's character is not even allowed coffee because of his sales record.

What I love about this movie is that all of the salespeople are working the same leads. One of them is doing extremely well and making sales, while the other three are complaining and bitching about the quality of their leads. The complaining and bitching scenes are incredibly well done, and I think you will identify with them. I used to have these types of discussions with my colleagues in my early years of selling. The scene that I especially enjoy is the one with Ed Harris and Alan Arkin when they are having a cup of coffee at their restaurant hangout, talking about "the leads." The nuance of their language and the back and forth is so realistic.

Rant Alert! Glengarry Glen Ross illustrates one of my biggest problems with salespeople in general. They are always complaining, bitching and moaning about something. A lot of salespeople are great at finding fault with the company they work for, their manager, the software programs they use, the economy, other salespeople, or even the weather. Yes, I have personally known salespeople who have blamed their poor sales performance on the weather. Give me a break! I have learned over the years that it all starts with *you* and no one else. I am the one responsible for my sales success and no one else is. I am also the one who will benefit or suffer based on my performance. When I view my work and environment in a positive way, I can block out all of the potential problems and issues and in turn be successful.

Don't play the blame game, control your mind, stay positive and focused on what you need to do, and make sales happen. I will repeat this: *focus on what **YOU** need to do*. No one else is going to help you; it's all up to you. When you see other agents complaining about stuff, just pass them by and go to work on what you need to do. Movies such as *Glengarry Glen Ross*, this book, and other resources will help you see them for what they are: a simple distraction.

I have already discussed different types of marketing activities you need to focus on in your first year. Your precious time should be spent working on these projects, not complaining about "the leads" or anything else. Let's take a "Time Management Quiz" and see how you score. Write down your choices as you go. Answers will be at the end of the quiz along with a grading scale.

Choose between the two activities listed. Which is a better use of your time, Option A or Option B?

Number 1:

Option A: Accepting an invitation to a Broker Open House, which includes a free lunch, in a neighboring city where you don't work as much.
Option B: Go to lunch with a past work colleague at a company where you worked together for two years.

Number 2:

Option A: Attend the monthly office meeting.
Option B: Review an Inspection Report with your buyer. The Inspection Notice is due the next day.

Number 3:

Option A: Attend a leads group meeting for the first time.
Option B: Go preview three new listings in your target market.

Number 4:
Option A: Write two blog posts about a new listing you just got and a closing you had the day before.
Option B: Go to lunch with a couple of the other agents in your office.

Number 5:
Option A: Go to a seminar in the morning discussing "Cold Calling Techniques in the 21st Century."
Option B: Go to the gym for your workout.

Number 6:
Option A: Go to lunch with a past client. You just closed on their house last month.
Option B: Go to a local Chamber of Commerce meeting discussing networking strategies.

Number 7:
Option A: You've worked the past two weekends. Your colleague asks you to host an open house for one of her listings on Sunday.
Option B: You've worked the past two weekends. Your kids want you to take them to zoo on Sunday.

Number 8:
Option A: Your monthly date night with your spouse or significant other.
Option B: Your local Realtor Association has a get together at one of the local restaurants.

Number 9:
Option A: Free lunch at a local park sponsored by the mortgage broker in your office.
Option B: Lunch with one of your past clients.

Number 10:
Option A: Big Motivational Day Speaker Event conducted at a large hotel in the City.
Option B: Morning hike in the mountains by yourself.

Here are the answers:
1.   B (Broker Open Houses outside of your territory are a waste of time.)
2.   B (This is easy. The Inspection review is a direct sales activity.)
3.   B (Previews are valuable and keep you in tune with the market.)
4.   A (Lunch with other agents usually turn into bitch sessions, avoid at all costs!)
5.   B (Get your workout in. Cold calling techniques are not as critical anymore.)
6.   A (Local Chamber meetings are not effective in my opinion.)
7.   B (Balance your life and make time for your kids.)
8.   A (Very easy, keep "the Boss" at home happy. Local Realtor events are mainly socially oriented.)
9.   B (Keep networking with past clients. This is one of the best uses of your time.)
10. B (Motivational speaking events usually turn into advertising days for coaching programs, etc. Avoid them! Unless it's a speaker you are really interested in seeing in person.)

1-5 correct: You need to read this book at least three more times before you start managing your time.

6-9 correct: You are on the right track! Good job.

10 correct: Stop reading this book right now and start working! You are ready. :)

Chapter 21
Create a Positive Real Estate Experience

One of my goals as a real estate agent is to create a "Positive Real Estate Experience" for my clients. I want my clients to feel good about the transaction we completed. I want them to also feel good about me as their real estate agent and the experience we shared during the process. That way, when time goes by, they have happy and positive memories of the purchase or sale of their home and of me as their real estate agent.

Think back to one of your most recent large purchases, a car, house, engagement ring, or even a high-end, expensive restaurant. Most times if you had a positive experience, it was because the salesperson did a good job and made you feel special while providing excellent service, advice, and counsel during the process.

I remember one time when my wife and I went to a four star restaurant to celebrate our wedding anniversary. Unfortunately, the experience was not a positive one for us, because we did not receive the service and attention we expected. At the restaurant we did not order a bottle of wine for the two of us, so we felt that the waiter was upset with us. We were pressured to buy a bottle of wine by the sommelier, but we didn't feel comfortable drinking a bottle for just the two of us. We were then ignored by our waiter for long stretches of time after the bottle of wine incident. The memory of that bad experience is still vivid in my mind, and I am disappointed because I wanted to give my wife a special dinner that night and we didn't get it. This happened over ten years ago and I still harbor bad feelings.

A positive example for me is when I bought our engagement ring. Like most men, I had no idea whatsoever about diamonds, how much to spend, or what my wife would want. I knew someone who was a jeweler and he did a fantastic job helping us. He specifically helped my wife pick out the diamond ring that was right for her. He was very patient and did not pressure us, which I appreciated because my wife needs time to make decisions. My wife and I both enjoyed the process because the jeweler made it fun for us. He provided the right information in order to make the perfect choice. Nine years later, my wife and I are still happy about the ring and look back fondly on our experience of buying it together.

These were two separate situations, and two completely different experiences were created by the person providing the service. One was negative and unhappy, and the other was positive, fun and satisfying. The memory of each experience will stay with me for the rest of my life. Memories are quirky things. Usually, what people remember most and for the longest period of time is how they felt in a particular situation. They will be vocal about both good and bad experiences, basing recommendations and referrals solely on their memories of these feelings. We have not been back to that restaurant since that night, and I have not recommended it to any of my friends or clients. As you can imagine, I have referred many people to the jeweler who we bought our engagement ring from, and I have gone back many times to buy other gifts from him.

When someone buys or sells their house, the experience and the memories stay with them forever. In today's challenging economic climate, people will buy or sell a home much less frequently than in the past. Because much more is at stake, their expectations are much higher. My goal is to make sure that all my clients have a "Positive Real Estate Experience" so they will have happy memories of the sale or purchase of their home. At the same time, they will have good feelings and memories of me as their real estate agent.

How do I do this? I give my clients outstanding service, I am honest at all times, and I make it a point to have fun during the process. This way my clients call me back for repeat business and refer me to their friends and family. Maya Angelou may have said it best:

"People will forget what you said, people will forget what you did, but people will never forget how you made them feel."

Chapter 22
Strategies for Working With Buyers, Sellers and Agents

This chapter piggybacks on the last by giving you specific strategies for creating a "Positive Real Estate Experience." I will go into tactics that apply when you are representing buyers or sellers. The final section focuses on how to work successfully with other real estate agents, which will become a big part of your job.

Five Strategies for Working With Buyers

1) Don't Sell Them. My first tip here is don't try and "sell" a particular house to your buyers. They don't want you to do that, and it will hurt your relationship with them. Just tell your buyers the truth about each house you view. Explain the benefits and features of each house in a matter of fact way. At the same time, explain the potential problems and issues with each house you view. For example, if the neighborhood has a high number of rentals, you need to tell your buyers regardless of the implications. Perhaps you are aware that windows in this neighborhood are problematic and don't function well. My concrete heaving example from Chapter 7 applies here, as well. Just tell your clients what you know. They are going to find out about any problems or issues related to a house at some point, so it's best if they hear it from you. Tell them up front what you know and they will appreciate your honesty. Your buyers will also value your opinion because you are offering them real value with your expertise.

2) Get Your Sleuth On: Become Sherlock Holmes. The famous detective once said, "when you have eliminated the impossible, whatever remains, however improbable, must be the truth." When working with buyers, it is a good idea to go through a process of elimination together. I have found that when buyers actually go out and see more homes, *especially* ones they don't like at all, it helps them choose the house they really want. It locks them in on "the one" because they have taken the time and effort to view all of the possibilities. It is hard work and it does take time for you as the real estate agent, but it is worth it because the buyers have made the choice themselves based on what they have seen. You get to play "detective" and learn more about what your clients' true desires are (even when they themselves do not know!), enabling you to serve them better.

Let's say you and your buyers have identified a list of 20 homes that are possibilities. Do you think it's a good idea for you to view the 20 homes first to screen them further for your buyers? After you view the 20 homes, you could pick out the top five for your buyers. This way, you will save your clients a lot of time by narrowing the list down to five homes. You would have more time on the visit to view the city and other landmarks in the area.

Of course this makes sense from a practical standpoint. But from a sales standpoint, it's a terrible idea. Your clients want and need to be involved in the entire process of viewing the homes. This is what they look forward to the most. It's going to be their house, and they want to see all the possible houses that meet their criteria. This way, they won't miss out on "the one."

I know a lot of agents who *do* feel it's their responsibility to preview and screen houses for their buyers. I do not believe in this strategy at all. I have helped a lot of buyers who are moving to my area from out of state or even from outside the country. Together with these buyers, I coordinate a house hunting trip. They visit the area for at least two or three days to view properties and get to know the area better. Most times, the buyers want to write an offer on the house of their choice on their first visit so they can start coordinating their move.

By removing types of houses and areas they do not like (the impossible), the buyers will discover the types of houses and areas which they do like (the truth). It's a process your buyers have to go through themselves; you can't do it for them. They need to reach their choice with you at their side helping them. You will point out the pluses and minuses of each house and neighborhood, while playing "detective" and using your powers of observation to get to know your clients better. You don't need to sell or promote any of the houses because your buyers will arrive at the truth on their own.

3) Work Your Way Up the Price Ladder. Whenever possible, schedule home viewing tours with buyers starting with the lowest priced homes. Work your way up the price ladder to the highest priced homes. This way buyers can see that the most expensive homes are not necessarily the best. I always point out to my buyers the importance of finding a house or houses with the most value based on price. Value and price do not go hand in hand when viewing homes. If a house is priced $50,000 more than another, it does not necessarily mean the higher priced home is far superior. By showing homes going up the price ladder you can illustrate this point to your buyers.

I have found it helpful to end the tour with the home that I feel is the best fit for the buyers regardless of price based on their buying criteria. The most expensive home, usually, is not going to be the best fit for your clients. By scheduling the tour in this manner, it helps the buyers make a choice. Most times buyers end up liking the last house I show them because it fits most of their hot buttons based on my research and preparation. Plus, emotions become stronger at the end of a tour and the buyers latch on to the last house, so that's why I try to show them the nicest home last based on what they want.

Ideally, at the end of long house hunting tour you want your buyers to have one house which they really, really like.

4) Kill Them With Kindness. Always speak positively about a house your buyer has interest in with the listing agent or seller if the house is a FSBO (For Sale by Owner). Sellers are extremely emotional about their home simply because it's *their home*.

I have seen much better responses from sellers on my client's offer when I take the time and effort to praise the nice features of the seller's home.

5) Let Them Make Their Own Decisions. If your buyer is lukewarm about a house and wants to wait until a more suitable one comes on the market, continue to help them with their search. When representing buyers on their offer price, provide the buyer with the information they need to make a reasonable offer price, but don't push them to arrive at a specific price point. Pushing clients into making decisions will inevitably damage your relationship with them. Although the success of the transaction does impact your income as a real estate agent, you are not party to the transaction and certainly have less at stake. Clients will value and appreciate the patience you show them; they never want to feel they have been manipulated or pushed into making a decision, especially such a large one. As real estate agents, we have a responsibility *to* our clients, but we never can nor should attempt to make decisions *for* our clients.

Six Strategies for Working With Sellers

1) Have a Plan. Above all, when you are representing the seller, have a plan in place for how you will sell the house. Each house is going to have its own unique features and challenges, so you need to communicate to the seller your plan on marketing and selling their house.

2) Manage Expectations. The days of getting a listing and just planting the "For Sale" sign in the front yard are over. If you promise that you can sell a house in 60 days at a specific price, you may be setting yourself up for failure. Most sellers today are looking for a full service listing arrangement where you actually market the house in addition to just having it plugged into the MLS. Sophisticated sellers today expect home staging services, professional photography, online virtual tours, mailers, and online visibility on social media websites. I am not saying that all sellers expect this, but I feel that in the future more and more sellers will expect a higher level of service.

3) Be Honest With Your List Price Recommendation. This piggybacks and really is part of managing expectations with your sellers, but I feel so strongly about this that I decided to give it its own heading. When talking to sellers about listing their house, I am always honest about providing sales comparables and coming up with a recommended price. I do not feel it's in my best interest to flatter them and overstate what I feel the house will sell for, because then I have to live with their false expectation. I *have* lost listings because other agents promised the seller their house would sell at a price much higher than what the market would bear. In these cases, I watched to see what the house sold for. More often than not, the house ended up selling at the price point I had recommended from the beginning. I know I could use false promises to get more listings, but I just can't do it!

4) Communicate, Don't Deliberate. Your seller values constant contact from you, and the information you provide will help them make decisions about the sale of their home. Even if you do not have anything new to report, give them a call and tell them so. They need to hear from you frequently and know you are working for them. If things are not going well, talk to your sellers and let them know what is happening. For example, if there have not been any showings over an extended period of time, your seller needs to know. A price reduction may or may not be necessary depending on local market conditions. Monitor your listing's competition; that is, pay attention to what is happening to comparable homes for sale in the neighborhood. If other houses are going under contract, a price reduction might be a good solution. But don't deliberate. Again, be mindful to always leave decisions up to your client. Give them the information they need and always let them come to their own conclusion. I have found it best to never make decisions for any of my clients.

5) First Things First: Get a Home Inspection. Get a home inspection completed before the property goes on the market. Especially in a down market, it's best to identify potential problems at the outset. This will prevent a lot of negotiation with the buyer once you are under contract. In the end, this will save big headaches for your clients because they will be prepared to address whatever problems exist. They will anticipate any buyer objections, and won't have to give in so much on the inspection resolution. This may even help them to be more realistic about their price.

6) Qualify the Buyer's Lender. Due to the proliferation of less-than-reputable lenders, this is more important today than ever. Will the buyer and lender be able to complete the closing? Will the money be there at the closing table? Over time, you will get to know the lenders in your area, but at first you may have to do some research or ask around. If at all possible, try to make sure the buyer is using a local lender.

Practical Advice for Working With Other Agents

One of the hardest parts of my job is being dependent on the real estate agent on the other side of a deal. Over the years, I have had my share of run-ins with other agents. I can't count how many times I have been lectured by other real estate agents during my career. They say things such as, "I have been a Realtor for 32 years, do you know what you are doing?" As a new agent, don't take this one too personally. In fact, whenever I get the comment about how many years *they* have been in the business, I know I am doing a good job and keeping them on their toes.

You'll work with all different types of agents, so be prepared for anything. Some are absolutely excellent and very professional. Some are working part-time and impossible to get in touch with by phone or email. Just keep your clients informed of what is going on. They should be aware of the challenges you are facing if you end up having to work with an unprofessional real estate agent.

Most agents are great to work with, but you will have a few who will be a challenge. Be strong and don't be intimidated by other real estate agents. Just remember that you work for your client and not the other agent and you'll be fine.

Chapter 23
The Future Real Estate Agent

The real estate industry is going through major changes right now, and the up-heaval is causing a lot of long-time agents to get out of the business for good. This is leaving room for new, younger agents, and agents with experience in other industries to enter the marketplace.

The old school real estate agents of the past are no longer valued by the public. Their old fashioned sales methods are a turnoff to the more informed Internet generation of buyers and sellers. The advice I got from experienced agents when I started in the business simply didn't work for me.

This means that you have the opportunity to set yourself apart by being the type of real estate agent that consumers value and want. New agents today have a huge advantage over "old school" agents who have been in business for many years. You understand and embrace technology better than your predecessors. Your past experience in another industry might give you perspective or an insight others are missing. Above all, you have no baggage from the past and you are open-minded about creating your business to meet the demands of the public.

Here are ten ways you can set yourself apart from the competition, both from the "old school" agents of the past, and other agents of the future like you.

1) Honesty Will Rule the Day. By now, I hope you understand how valuable it will be to you to always be honest with your clients and yourself. Over time it gets easier. Your pipeline will grow, and you will close more and more deals. You will realize that your livelihood is not dependent on closing that "one deal" all the time. Still, keep this in mind as you are starting out, and you will set yourself apart from your competition.

2) Connect With All Types of People. Who are you? Tap into your background. Travel and meet new people. All different types of people from all over the world are buying houses now, and you need to be able to build relationships with them.

3) Understand Public Relations. The online world is part of everyone's lives. Computers, smartphones, portable computers, and pretty soon TVs will all be integrated with the Internet. "Screen time" is now a part of our daily lives. Real estate agents who understand this and promote themselves online are the ones who will succeed. Promote yourself professionally, and focus on your achievements. Your sphere wants to see you do well, and they will cheer you on.

4) Do It "Your Way." Listen to Frank Sinatra sing his classic song "My Way" and you will be inspired to follow this piece of advice. I have been in sales all of my professional life. One thing I have learned is that the best way for me to sell and help my clients is to do it my way. One of my strategies early on as a real estate agent was to trust my instincts and treat my clients the way I would want to be treated. I tapped into the feelings I had when I bought my first home, and did my best to provide service to my clients based on what I had wanted.

One of the great things about being a real estate agent is that there is no right or wrong way to do business, particularly on how you market yourself. What works for one agent might not work for another. Have confidence in yourself. Trust yourself and do it your way. I did it my way, and so can you.

5) Think Long Term. Remember that in most cases, you want to do business with and help your customers more than once. Your success is dependent on repeat business and referrals. Always be looking to the future and be sure to cultivate referrals from past customers. If you think short-term, you will not succeed. Your goal is to have your customers for life: from their first house to when they move up to a bigger house, maybe buy an investment property or two, and then downsize to a smaller house at some point. Along the way, your customers need to be providing you with referrals, which turn into more customers for life.

6) Rely on Your Expertise, Not Your Refrigerator Magnets. People will want to work with you based on your expertise, knowledge, and the value you offer them. I don't understand why real estate agents are still sending out cheesy knick-knack type items like refrigerator magnets! The days of sending out junk mail to a global list are over. Sending things to past and current clients is okay, just don't mail it out to a huge mailing list of people you are not working with or have never met. Your reputation will suffer. Your success is more about who you are and what you know, not what you mail out to people.

7) Make It Your Lifelong Pursuit. Successful agents are committed to their career as a lifelong endeavor. They see themselves as professionals and they love their job. They understand the "snowball effect" and how year after year they are going to generate more business from past clients through repeat business and referrals. When you view yourself this way, your clients will have confidence in you. They see you as a professional real estate agent, not just someone who is working part time trying to make a few bucks on the side.

Professional real estate agents are continually building their skills. They are attending continuing education courses in real estate to keep their license active. Professional agents are always focused on getting better so they can be more effective when helping their clients.

Value is what clients want, not a firm handshake and cheesy smile that has no substance. The future real estate agent will have confidence in who they are and what they do because they have the expertise and knowledge their clients need. They realize that it's about gaining respect from their clients because their clients value them.

8) Be an Advisor, Not a Salesperson. Think of yourself as an advisor, not a salesperson. People want to buy, but they don't want to be sold. They want someone to help them make the right choice. Create a presence with your service and personality by being an excellent listener.

9) Be Yourself, Have Fun, and Give Back. It may sound cliché, but remember to always be thankful, appreciate all you have, and don't be consumed by your work. If you enjoy your job and have fun doing it, your clients will enjoy working with you. It can be a serious business buying or selling a home. A little levity and a positive attitude will help your clients relax and enjoy the process as best they can, given their situation.

Get involved with community projects, volunteer work, and local schools. In addition to being a real estate agent, have a life! Follow your bliss, whatever it might be: traveling, teaching, painting, writing, or speaking. Expand your horizons and it will naturally lead to a deeper connection with your customers based on some of your hobbies and activities. Plus, you will be a happier person overall.

10) Build Equity in Yourself and Your Business. As a real estate agent, you are building a business for yourself. The snowball effect happens over time with repeat business and referrals. Your skills and expertise will also improve the longer you are in business. Don't keep doing the same thing over and over again each year. Learn from the previous year by always building your knowledge and skills. Take a realistic inventory, and keep doing the things that are working. Change the things that aren't.

Chapter 24
Don't Give Up

There will come a point in your career as a real estate agent where your spouse, significant other, or partner (if you have one) will become concerned during one of your slow periods and quiz you about your job. Sometimes it will be direct, and other times it can be indirect. Here are some examples of what you might hear:

- "Have you considered going back to what you were doing before real estate?"
- "Do you miss working at your old job?"
- "I don't think you are going to make the amount of commissions you expected to."
- "You are not being realistic. You can't make a living this way. You've only had a few closings over the past six months!"

These are very difficult conversations, and they can put a strain on your relationship. I know how hard it is because I have had these kinds of conversations with my wife over the years. She is not a salesperson; she's an engineer. In the beginning, it was hard for her to understand the peaks and valleys of a true commission sales job. For me, it was tough in the beginning because my business is somewhat seasonal; I have always been busier in the spring and summer. By the time December rolls around I hear, "anything new today?" from "the Boss" at home quite often. Sometimes days and weeks can go by before I get a new opportunity or client. The slow times can be quite stressful for both of you. I have found that the best strategy is to reassure your spouse or partner that the slow times are only temporary. You will get more business and you can't walk away from what you have already been building with your business.

Never, ever give up! I wish I could write this a million times for emphasis! This is the most important message I can give you when you are starting out in your career as a real estate agent, and it's the most important message I have given in this book. You *will* be pressured by those closest to you to quit at some point in the future. So never, ever give up!

The best thing about the slow times is that the busy times always follow. Just like the seasons, winter is always followed by spring. The flowers bloom, the grass turns green, and the trees fill in with their beautiful leaves. The same is always true for sales if you stay focused and work hard during the slow times. The snowball will keep growing until it brings you an avalanche of new business. If you quit or get distracted, the whole system breaks down. So stay busy and never give up during the slow times and new business will come. I say this with absolute confidence because it has happened to me so many times in my sales career.

Have you ever watched a house being built? The foundation goes in first, and seems to take a lot of time! The architect and builders have to plan and make sure they are building a solid foundation. It's hard work, for sure. What if they quit after building the foundation? Most of the hard work is already done, but the house is just sitting there with no second floor because they gave up. Would a builder ever do this? Of course not! There is too much at stake. So never, ever give up. You are building a business; it takes time, and you have to stick with it.

Believe me; it does get easier with time. I have been in business as a real estate agent now for over nine years. The level of repeat business and referrals are much higher than they were in my first few years. I have built something valuable for myself and I am proud of it. You can do the same if you stick with it. The fruits of your labor, creativity, and hard work will always pay off. The beauty of sales is, unlike many other professions, you reap what you sow.

What do you want to do with your life? Everyone is always searching for something because we all feel something better is just around the corner. When I look back on my life, I know that if I had started out in real estate right after college I would not have been successful. To be successful in some jobs, you need a sense of life perspective and experience. I definitely needed more structure as a recent college graduate, and the sales jobs I had for the fifteen years prior to becoming a real estate agent provided that structure. I also learned valuable sales skills, and developed a hunger to do something on my own during my fifteen years working a traditional, corporate sales job. I now appreciate being on my own so much more and would not trade it for the world. My perspective and experience prepared me to go out on my own successfully.

How about you? Where are you now in your life? Are you really ready to go out on your own and be a real estate agent? After reading this book, do you have a better perspective of what it's going to take to be successful? Do you have a passion to succeed at all costs? Can you put your clients' needs ahead of your own?

People are always talking about having a job that means something, where you are actually making a difference in the world or for someone. A real estate agent is helping their clients with their homes and through the biggest financial transaction most people make in their lives. This is significant because, when done correctly, you are truly helping your clients make a better life for themselves. When done incorrectly, you can actually ruin someone's life.

Given the recent mortgage foreclosure crisis in our country, as a real estate agent, you truly *can* make a difference. "Blame" is a tricky thing when discussing this topic. Some of the people who lost their homes in our country's mortgage meltdown knew what they were doing when they got second and third mortgages, and are responsible for their own plight. Unforeseen and unregulated financial instruments used on Wall Street also played a part. Based on what I have seen and read over the years, a lot of real estate agents were involved in criminal, borderline criminal, and dishonest activities. There have been many people put out on the street because of crooked or greedy real estate agents, builders, appraisers, and mortgage representatives. Consumers looked to these agents with trust and respect and how were they rewarded? Many of them lost their homes.

As real estate agents, we are here to help our clients, not screw them! Sorry for being graphic, but this is one of my motivations every day. I make a difference for my clients, and I add real value to their lives. This makes me proud of what I do for a living, and no one can take that away from me. This job can get very stressful and tedious; it's a lot of hard work. In the end, I always feel good about who I am because I know in my heart I am always focused on the best interests of my clients. If you take this seriously, you too can make a difference in the lives of your clients.

So when you are up late at night sweating and asking yourself, "when is that next closing going to happen?" or during your next argument with your spouse about money, think about what you do for a living. You are needed, and you can make the world a better place. I believe I was destined to become a real estate agent, and it's the best job I have ever had in my life. I love what I do and I am good at it, and that's a rare combination! I wish this for you as well, and I hope this book can help you on your journey. Let's do it together! My best wishes to you for a successful career.

Thank You
Mario Jannatpour
Realtor

Appendix A
Other Real Estate Agent Stories

Michael James, Michael Saunders & Company (Sarasota, Florida)

How and why did you get into real estate?
I entered real estate in my early 30s. I had just moved to Sarasota and it was time for a new career. My only regret is I did not find this career sooner.

I grew up in Toronto, and was expected to get a university degree and find a career in a large industry with a large corporate employer. Real estate did not even flash on my radar as a possibility. At the time, I did not consider it a viable career. My impression of Realtors came from the cheesy advertising I would see on bus stop benches and print media. They looked like egotistical, celebrity wannabes to me. What I did not know at the time was that beyond these flashy publicity seekers was another side to the business. A less visible, more professional group of Realtors that offered a very important service, performed with dignity and with their customer's best interests at heart.

After obtaining my degree, I entered the 8 to 5 corporate world and though the money was good, I was unfulfilled. The hardest part for me was having such a regimented lifestyle and only two weeks per year vacation. I found it all very stifling, as my whole life revolved around my job and the need to please my boss.

After a number of years I resigned and went travelling, eventually settling in Sarasota, Florida. The year was 1997 and by now I was wise enough to know that I wanted to have more control over my time while still making a good living. Real estate offered the perfect fit.

I obtained my real estate license right away and joined one of the large national companies as they offered good training and support. I immediately took to the freedom and was able to set my own schedule which at first was both a blessing and a curse.

I also enjoyed the potential for large paydays. I live in an area with many expensive, waterfront homes and there is always the possibility of a million dollar sale and the big commissions that come with it.

After a few years I was invited to join the number one company in town, one that is locally owned and has the most prestigious reputation. There are no tacky pseudo-celebrities in this group and my early image of what a Realtor is has changed for good.

What do you enjoy most about being a real estate agent?
What I love most about the business is the combination of high income potential and being able to set my own schedule. There is really no boss to answer to except myself. As long as I am producing for myself, I am producing for the company and my "job" is safe. I have two kids in elementary school and never miss a performance or award presentation. I can come home for lunch, I can work late one day and leave early the next. It's all up to me.

Of course there is a down side to any job where you are not paid a salary. The years 2007 through 2009 were very tough as sales activity took a nose dive. The biggest lesson the Realtor community learned is to save, save, save when times are good.

What is your niche or area of specialty?
Through the years I have developed a niche representing buyers moving to the area or buying a second home here. I find these buyers in many ways; from referrals from friends and past clients, from the web, from open houses, floor time, sign calls and referrals from my company. I have not found one magic source for new clients; instead I use a variety of approaches. I have also gained a reputation for being an effective listing agent. Listings bring buyer inquiries and it is always good to represent sellers as well. If I could do one thing better, it would be to develop a more efficient system for keeping in touch with people in order to get more referrals.

What is one thing which has made you successful?
I attribute my success to being a people person and to the sales training I received in the corporate world. In order to help people, there has to be an exchange of money at the closing table. Without a closing nobody gets paid including you. You have to keep your eyes on the prize and ask yourself consistently if what you are doing is contributing toward a successful closing. This includes politely turning down bad leads that only drain you of time and money.

One piece of advice for new agents?
My one piece of advice for new agents is to focus on time management and put in the hours to be successful. Remember it will take some time to develop a reliable stream of income. Go into the office frequently and show your face. Connect with the most successful agents and establish a reputation for enthusiasm and a willingness to learn. Be patient, stay positive and good things will surely come your way.

Jeff Rising, Foundation Realty (Adrian, MI)

How and why did you get into real estate?

I had wanted to be in real estate since I was 13 when my parents bought a home. I overheard them discussing what a real estate agent makes in commissions. It seemed like "easy money" in the mind of a teenager and I was also intrigued that someone could make a career out of helping people buy and sell homes. When I graduated from high school I went straight into factory work because at the time in Southeast Michigan it was supposedly the most stable job you could get, working for one of the big 3 automakers or a supplier. I bounced around to a couple of different auto supplier manufacturers, made it to a supervisory position by the time I was 26, but I just wasn't happy.

I left the car industry and took a couple of retail management jobs and eventually got my real estate license and I started working part time in real estate. I soon found out that working part time wouldn't cut it. I needed to put in a full time effort. I spent the next 5 years working as a licensed assistant for different real estate agents at a couple of different companies and found myself feeling unsatisfied with that role as well, I knew I wanted to be my own agent showing and selling homes.

I took the big jump in 2007 and went to work at RE/MAX Irish Hills to use the REO and foreclosure experience I gained from my previous job to start an REO department there. In 2007, I closed 4 transactions, and in 2008 I closed 80 and I have been doing quite well since. I am now focusing on helping homeowners avoid foreclosure either through modification or short sale. While working REO's is a necessary part of the market right now, my long term goal is to help neighborhoods retain property values through successful short sales and helping homeowners end up in a position so they can purchase a home again in 2-3 years after they get back on their feet.

What do you enjoy most about being a real estate agent?

I really enjoy working with people and helping them solve their problems. Whether their problem is that they think they can't sell and get what they want, or sell at all in this market, or they have been tirelessly searching for homes on their own online and just not getting anywhere. For me it all comes together at the closing table and you know you've succeeded when the client is thanking you for a job well done.

What is your niche or area of specialty?

Just as the market moves, your niche needs to move accordingly. Right now I am still listing a good number of foreclosures but I am really focusing on transitioning that to helping homeowners in distress through loan modification education and assisting them with a short sale if that is the only option for them.

What is one thing which has made you successful?
The one thing I hear over and over again from clients is that they are completely surprised how easy I am to get a hold of and that I call them back almost immediately, if I miss their call. I think communication is the key to a satisfied client. You need to know what your client's preferred method of contact is, by phone, email, social media or text, and stay on top of it. Even if you don't have any news at all on their listing, or any new homes for them to see, contact them anyway.

One piece of advice for new agents?
Funny you ask. I was thinking this morning that I could teach a class on "Professionalism" at my local Board of Realtors for new agent orientation. I think it's important to be professional, courteous and show integrity. We are professionals on the level of attorneys, doctors and accountants, and many of us make just as much money or more, but get the least respect in the community. The reason is that many real estate agents take this up as a "hobby" or "just doing this to help friends and family" or "I wanted to sell my own house and not pay commission" and don't take the work seriously. If that's your goal you are not likely to succeed. Real estate agents get a bad rap. I believe it's important for new agents to take the job seriously, work hard and serve their clients well.

Liz Caraway, REALTY EXECUTIVES (Seattle, Washington)

How and why did you get into real estate?
I had been working for about six years as a construction flagger and one afternoon while I was working......WHAM! I was hit by a driver going over 35mph. He plowed through my leg, throwing me up into his windshield...breaking it with my head and body, then over the top...hitting my head again on his luggage rack and then falling behind the car onto the pavement. Luckily, there wasn't anyone following him or I would have been run over by the second vehicle.

I was knocked out immediately and didn't wake up again until long after my surgery to reconstruct my shattered leg. I was in the hospital for over two weeks before they felt they could let me go home. My leg was supposed to heal within 3 months but it ended up being over a year and another surgery to do bone grafting to the shattered pieces. I ended up being handicapped for over two years. Wheel chair to Walker to Cane to Feet.

As soon as I was strong enough and able to walk with a cane comfortably (bones still broken inside!) I entered into the local Community College......getting around all the kids with my cane! For the next two years I studied and healed...graduating with almost a 4 point, on the Dean's list and earning an Associate's Degree in Marketing.

When I started trying to find an entry level Marketing job, I saw that there were few and with very low pay. Also, the staff and managers were all 20 years or more younger than me! Then I remembered my interest in real estate that I had back before I had kids. Everything about it was something I enjoyed doing AND a great deal of it was…guess…MARKETING!

At the same time I was in a Bible study and I had asked for prayers for my job search and the idea of going into real estate. Afterwards, one of the other women in the group came up to me and told me that her husband was a Managing Broker and was about to open his own office. I took this as a big "YES" from God and became his first agent at his new office.

I started back in 2001. I have been a National Award Winning Realtor almost every year I have been in the business.

What do you enjoy most about being a real estate agent?
Almost everything! I enjoy helping first time homeowners get their first home. Also, the independence to do anything I want to do.

What is your niche or area of specialty?
Through the years, I have worked mostly with homebuyers. But I have the following designations:

CRS (Certified Residential Specialist)
ABR (Accredited Buyer Representative)
SRES (Seniors Real Estate Specialist)
LHMS (Luxury Home Marketing Specialist)
GMS (Global Mobility Specialist)
TRC (Transnational Referral Certification)
The last few years, I've been trying to network into being a Relocation Specialist.

What is one thing which has made you successful?
My ability to start a conversation with anyone at anytime. I am never too shy to say something quirky like "Please tell me you're looking to buy a house or a condo!"

One piece of advice for new agents?
Start joining a lot of clubs to meet more people. Buy business cards for several different types of client. (buyer cards, seller cards, renter cards) Get over any shyness you may have, learn to talk about anything, "that's a nice coat" "awesome day today" "wow, you must be hungry"

Start to write a "Service Provider Directory." Then call EVERYONE you know and ask them for referrals that you can include in your directory like window washer, house cleaner, painter and then ask them their permission to include their name as the contributor. Ask if they want a copy of the finished product. Then you say, "Oh, by the way, do you know anyone that could use the help of a good Realtor?"

Then you call the service provider and do the same thing with them, connect and network with them!

Andrea Martone, RE/MAX First Choice (Parsippany,NJ)

How and why did you get into real estate?
I was very picky when looking for my own home and learned a lot throughout the year long process. The real estate agent I was working with at the time was the owner of that RE/MAX office and asked if I would like to train and come to work with her. I couldn't pass up the opportunity of being trained.

What do you enjoy most about being a real estate agent?
Happy clients! Especially when sellers receive a good offer for their home or when buyers close on the house they wanted and the process goes smoothly. Nothing feels better than helping people with the American dream, and when all is said and done they know they worked with an agent they could trust.

What is your niche or area of specialty?
Negotiations and marketing are my specialties. I have always had a strong ability to read people which really helps me negotiate the best deal for my seller or buyer. In marketing, I love coming up with ideas that are unique and stand out from the crowd.

What is one thing which has made you successful?
Being able to read people. I find that really listening to people and understanding what they want is the key to my success! Sometimes you also have to listen for what is not being said.

One piece of advice for new agents?
Never make it about the commission. Always do what is best for the customer. If you always put your client first, more clients will come. Never work out of desperation for a paycheck, you have to put people first, and that is the way to build a reputation and future.

Jean Griswold, Provident Living, Inc. (Piedmont, NC)

How and why did you get into real estate?
I was an entrepreneur in the healthcare industry for 20+ years before the industry and the major companies were divested. When my mother (now age 92) first

moved in with us, we had great difficulty finding a competent real estate agent to handle her very unique property (she had lived in the same home for 50 years). I finally decided that I could do a better job taking care of her personal situation if I got my license and helped her sell the property—never thinking that it would become a second career! I listed her property on 22 December; sold it for full price on 24 December (2 days on market)…and haven't looked back since.

What do you enjoy most about being a real estate agent?
I love working with sellers! Establishing the correct price point, evaluating all the nuances of each property's uniqueness, developing the marketing programs, strategizing how best to position the property for maximum views/hits—it gives me great satisfaction to take a seller through the entire process from reviewing all the components that go into making the decision that selling **IS** indeed what they want or need to do through a successful closing.

What is your niche or area of specialty?
I never intended to become a distressed property expert; however, the economic conditions in this market almost forced me to do so. Working with short sales led me to a relationship with the U.S. Bankruptcy Court locally, which has resulted in my becoming a bankruptcy Trustee listing agent. This means that when the Trustees for whom I work have a bankruptcy case that comes before them, if there is residential/commercial/land properties involved, I evaluate the properties and advise them on market conditions that will affect the sale of those properties. They then determine whether it is in the best interest of the estate for us to list the properties; if so, we list them, and the entire "seller's agent" process begins on behalf of the Trustee.

What is one thing which has made you successful?
Laser focus on the customer service aspect of the business—really listening to what the client needs, and developing a program that is client-specific to meet those needs. Our goal is to provide far better service than the client anticipates, and we have testimonials that confirm we are meeting that goal.

One piece of advice for new agents?
Don't try to straddle the fence of holding onto a "real job" while you are starting your real estate career; you can't truly be successful if you don't commit wholeheartedly to learning every single thing you can about the industry and implementing best practices into your own business. You are now a business owner; treat everything that you do as a full-time business.

Addy Saeed, RE/MAX Active Realty, Inc. (Toronto, Canada)

How and why did you get into real estate?
I remember coming to Canada when I was 17 and driving around with my family looking at houses with a real estate agent. The agent was courteous and had

immense knowledge of the local market as well as the houses we were seeing. He was able to articulate how a home would be a good fit. He also listened to what we were looking for and found the right home for our family. I was hooked! The lifestyle, the fast pace, the action! I went and registered for my courses when I was 19 to become a real estate agent.

What do you enjoy most about being a real estate agent?
I enjoy real estate for two reasons. It gives me the opportunity to measure what my potential is. The outcome I have in my business and my career is reliant on my commitment. The sharper my focus and my commitment, the easier the mundane tasks and higher returns. The second reason is the unique opportunity it provides for me to interact with the general public and helping my clients make possibly the biggest decision in their life. I love the dynamics a contract negotiation offers as well. I get a thrill when I can help my client save a dollar or help them get more for their property.

It's definitely a unique experience for me and I don't think I can ever substitute it for anything else…

What is your niche or area of specialty?
I have two areas in real estate that I specialize in and it's something that didn't come easy to me. I use to say that my niche was referrals. In 2010, 67% of my business was through referrals of friends and family hence working on anything from residential to industrial including investment properties. In mid 2010, I decided that I needed to create a niche in which I could service my clients better than anyone else could. This led me to making systematic changes in my business including setting up a referrals system with valuable agents that could be referred to in different areas allowing me to focus on my two core niche. Cabbagetown Homes (www.cabbagetowninfo.com) and Toronto Investment Properties (www.torontonianonline.com).

Cabbagetown is a neighborhood in Toronto that I reside in which is mainly focused around turn of the century homes that you could fall in love with over and over again. TorontonianOnline.com is based on my other love of finding properties to invest in. Wealth through real estate has been a dream of mine which I'm living!

What is one thing which has made you successful?
FOCUS! I remember driving on the highway thinking about how to achieve results that I would miss my exits. It sounds bad but I use that example all the time when I'm teaching because it's true. I've come up with some of my greatest ideas when I've been stuck in traffic. You have to be focused on what you want to achieve and take action. You have dreams, much like I do, and only way to get to them is to put some skin into it. If you don't know where you want to go, you will never get there. Focus on your target and take action to achieve them.

One piece of advice for new agents?

Be consistent and persistent! Constant effort will land you on your goal when you're least expecting it. Lead generation is a prime example. If you generate leads every day, you're bound to have high quality leads which will lead you to have a successful career because everything starts with leads. Once you're over that hurdle, everything else is easy! I'm astonished at how all real estate agents know this but not many choose to act on it. Be inspired and stay the course!

Find an accountability partner. This would be someone that is already achieving at a higher level than you are. If you want something that you haven't achieved, you need to do things that you haven't done yet. I found the easiest way for me to get inspired was to meet with a top producer in my office and picking their brain about how they are doing their business.

Loretta Jobs, Century 21 (Murray, KY)

I was a social worker and I could not close the door at the office at the end of the day and forget the needs of my clients. After working all day I could be called out late at night.

I thought being a real estate agent would give me flexibility with my time and office hours. Having a three year old and a six year old at the time I quickly learned the flexibilities of being a real estate agent was the right position for me with a family. The position allowed me to be at home when the children were sick or when I was needed at their school or being at home when they arrived home from school was the career for me. I have been able to set my own hours and work outside of the office. With technology my hours have become even more flexible and an office can really be portable or virtual.

Real estate has been fast paced and a rewarding career for me. I have gotten to make dreams come true for hundreds of families. I have gotten to meet people that I would have never met had I not been in real estate. They are my friends…. young and old. For some years now, I have enjoyed matching that perfect home with the young couple as their first home. That was fun and rewarding. And then as their families grew, I had the opportunity to sell their property and to find that perfect larger home for those same families. That was fun and rewarding.

Our town was designated the number 1 place to retire by Rand McNally. Finding and matching homes for retirees then became my niche. That was fun and rewarding too. "Empty nesters" or retirees, however, are found in any town.

To be successful in real estate an agent needs product knowledge, integrity, perseverance and commitment. So I obtained a few professional designations which taught me also the sales and communication skills. I found the perfect office for me which also provided real estate education.

I mentioned finding the right office is important. Our office works as a team. The agents in my office and the staff members have become my family away from home. I have really found that to be especially true this year. I have had some health issues and while I had surgery and chemotherapy my clients were taken care of by the other agents and the staff. I did not miss a commission!

Repeat sales and referrals are the life of the real estate business. After you have been in the real estate business for about three years I maintain that if you are not getting repeat sales and referrals from your satisfied clients, you need to adjust your service to your clients. This is a service business and it is your business….not just the company's business….not the just the Managing Broker's business….your business.

Being a real estate agent has given me the opportunity to invest in real estate. Since I am an investor in real estate, I not only have another avenue of income, I have credibility of counseling other investors. I invested in real estate for current income as well as for my retirement .

Being involved in my community and on my local real estate board have been positives for me in the real estate business. I have been active in my chamber of commerce, having served as President, active in Habitat for Humanity, an active Rotarian, volunteering at the hospital in the ER, serving on commissions at the First United Methodist Church to mention a few and this year establishing a satellite for Kids Against Hunger.

I have served in every office on my local real estate board and have served as an Associate Director for the Kentucky Real Estate Association. You need to develop a relationship with your fellow REALTORS. Remember they can also send you referrals.

My success can be summarized: "You can trust Loretta to provide the perfect balance of experience, market knowledge, and unexpected service."

Larry Lawfer, RE/MAX Landmark (Milton,MA)

How and why did you get into real estate?
I got into real estate emotionally when I was in my teens. With a friend we used to drive around Bucks County in Pennsylvania where I grew up to look at homes, buildings, offices and malls. We would talk about people's homes and why they lived in one neighborhood or another. We would wonder if we had lived in a different neighborhood and went to a different school, would we be different people? My friend Mark went on to become a very successful Commercial real estate agent

and is still active today. I took another route through Commercial Photography and Video Production and didn't really get into the business of real estate until after being hired by Mark. And afterwards I was hired by many other agents and agencies to produce marketing materials for their company and offerings.

In 2008, I was asked by an EXIT Realty franchise owner in Dallas, TX to create some testimonial marketing materials for his office. Our relationship continued through some 18 videos over the next couple of years. In January of 2010 I joined the firm as an agent and Director of Marketing. Over the next 9 months, I built the web presence of this firm and created many other videos which took them from the 7th page in Google searches to the first page in their select area. Unfortunately, for this firm my skills and lead generation couldn't overcome their haphazard and non-existent business strategy and implementation. I left the office in September, 2010 and joined RE/MAX Landmark in November. My experience in this new office is the exact opposite of what I had in EXIT. It is not because of the Brand, but Brand does have something to do with it, but it has everything to do with the systems, procedures and makeup of the people within the new office versus the other. I got into real estate because I am fascinated with family and home and community and architecture and design and marketing. There is no other better profession for my skills.

What do you enjoy most about being a real estate agent?
I think what I enjoy most is helping people achieve goals and objectives. I love being part of a team, maybe even team leader, who delivers on our goal. I like all the various details that have to be handled correctly. I love the story of house, home and family. This is the life's blood of our anthropology. Understanding a community through its homeowners and the homes they inhabit is fascinating every single day. The fact that I can get paid for my knowledge, expertise, energy and insight into this process is just the best of all possible worlds.

What is your niche or area of specialty?
I am not sure if I am experienced enough to say I have a niche. I feel as though I am comfortable with all aspects of what comes to me. I do REO, BPO work as well as service the luxury market. I know I am most passionate about great homes in great communities. Fortunately there is a lot of that in my immediate area. I expect a third of my business will be luxury homes, while the bulk of my work will be done in general residential real estate. Being in a high-end market around the Boston area, with our average home price in the $600,000 range I know from my Dallas experience that this is a great place to serve.

What is one thing, which has made you successful?
I think all successful agents have many skills. I pride myself on my ability to truly listen to what my clients are saying to me and building a vision of what they want

in my head. It is with their story and their vision in my head that I apply my professional skills to find, secure and close on that exact property. I think listening is my best skill, but my talent is in getting the job done.

One piece of advice for new agents?

From your first day on the job until your last look for, engage and learn from people around you who are working at the highest levels. Surround yourself with people who are successful and open and pay attention. Read great books, follow great systems.

With this focus on the positive I can also easily say the flip side is equally important. RUN from anyone who is negative, backbiting, gossipy or undermining, RUN and never look back.

Richie Alan Naggar, RAN Right Realty (Riverside, CA)

How and why did you get into real estate?

I worked for a person who owned three companies and one of them was a hard money lender. I saw the real estate agent getting some really nice checks while I did most of the work. I thought I should look into this. That was in 1978. Being a real estate agent was a pretty classy thing to be at that time. They dressed well, drove nice cars, and seemed to be happy making money. What's not to like?

What do you enjoy most about being a real estate agent?

The people contact and the different daily work episodes make for a satisfying balanced daily journey. Real estate allows you to travel and evolve while practicing it. The subject of real estate is so vast that your learning experience never ends. It is a never ending sea with no shores but plenty of islands to put into it.

What is your niche or area of specialty?

I am a seller's agent of Residential real estate. I have worked for buyers as well. However, buyers take up a lot of your time, so you should allow for that. I also liked real estate tract sales and selling for builders. In addition, I thoroughly enjoyed land assemblage and creating subdivisions. Now, consultations regarding Unlawful Detainers, property management, short selling, and foreclosures occupy my time.

What is one thing which has made you successful?

This may stun you, but I learned not to be greedy which is harder to do than you realize because you are battling with yourself when you are. I learned how to really do business when I discovered the win/win principals where everyone wins and not just me. Until that time, I made money but a lot of enemies too. That doesn't have to be that way. Now, I get happy seeing others prosper as well and I am grateful for that.

One piece of advice for new agents?

Make sure your skills bank lines up with this profession or you will hit all the uphill dirt roads and more difficult paths. Make sure you like people, can communicate and can finish what you start. Then, if you can insert generous amounts of charity (love) into what you are doing, you may have something worthy going. Money and escrows come and go, but learning to serve other people benefits you and others all the days of our lives. Don't base everything you do on money.

Susan Plage, RE/MAX of Boulder (Boulder, Colorado)

How and why did you get into real estate?

Real estate is my fourth career, having worked in education, advertising, and software development previously. I answered an ad for an Administrative Assistant to a real estate agent (Broker). It paid more than what I was making at the time, and that was my focus not the position.

If the truth be told, a career in real estate has eluded me for more than 20 years. Why? I really never saw it as a career path or a profession. It was something someone else did.

When I started real estate classes, I realized that all of my training led me to this fourth career.

What do you enjoy most about being a real estate agent (Broker)?

I am into puzzles, board games and the intrigue of problem solving. That plays well in the important decision-making process of real estate. It's search, seek, and acquire in basic terms.

In the world of real estate, that is what we do for the consumer: search the market for purchase options or listing comparables; seek the partner (buyer or seller) who will compliment the consumer's need, and acquire the intended result or a closing.

What is your niche or area of specialty?

My statistics include source of business, type of business and recurring business. Based on that, I am neither a right brain nor left brain; neither a listing broker nor buyer broker exclusively. My business is based on a consistent message to my relationship database and the opportunity that results.

Lately, strange to say in today's marketplace, I have thoroughly enjoyed my relationship with sellers. My presentation is realistic and my expectations for the process are based on market conditions as well as client need.

Buyers have always been a mainstay for my enthusiasm in real estate. Theirs is the puzzle that is to be solved.

What is one thing that has made you successful?
What my clients tell me: it's patience. What my coaches tell me: don't get attached to the outcome. What I tell myself: always be positive.

One piece of advice for new agents (Brokers)?
Think of real estate as a career path, and as a means to an end. It is a great source of satisfaction amidst pressures and uncertainty. It is a path that can bring you greater personal confidence; greater expectations of yourself. It can provide you, your partner and your family with a resourceful future.
It's not just something someone else does.

Margaret Woda, Long and Foster Real Estate (Crofton, MD)

How and why did you get into real estate?
When my husband graduated from Navy OCS and received PCS orders across country to a ship home-ported in San Diego, CA, I had very mixed feelings. It would be an adventure to live in another part of the country, but it also meant leaving my own first job as an elementary school music teacher.

I could not have imagined that schools in our destination city would have self-contained elementary school classrooms—i.e., no specialist teachers in the arts or physical education. Unable to put my music education degree to work, I got a job as a property manager for a real estate company to keep me occupied during my husband's 9-month deployment to Vietnam. The rest, as they say, is history.

What do you enjoy most about being a real estate agent?
The satisfaction of helping people achieve their real estate goals is a real "high" that stays with me for years after their closing. I feel like a proud momma bear when I hear about their job promotions, new babies, and children's accomplishments, knowing that I had a teeny role in helping them find the right neighborhood and the right home where their family would thrive. Being a professional REALTOR allows me an opportunity to touch so many people's lives in a positive way.

What is your niche or area of specialty?
My niche is residential real estate sales.
As the wife, daughter and granddaughter of veterans, helping military families address the challenges of PCS orders to and from Maryland is a very important segment of my business. Of course, I also enjoy helping civilian families with relocation and local families find a home to satisfy their changing needs.

What is one thing which has made you successful?

Success occurs when preparation meets opportunity, and that's certainly true when it comes to real estate. While there are many contributing factors to a successful real estate career, preparation is the one key ingredient that can't be overlooked. Detailed market reports, market trends analysis, and property reports are essential for both sellers and buyers. I don't take any shortcuts with this information.

One piece of advice for new agents?

"Practice, drill, and rehearse." From opening a lockbox to assembling a listing package…from reviewing forms with clients (knowing how to accurately summarize every paragraph of every form you might ever use) to handling incoming client calls and emails…practice, drill, and rehearse for family members, for your mentor, or anyone who will listen. And, if there's no one to listen, there's always your mirror or a pillow. Just do it so you'll be prepared to work with clients when the time comes.

Appendix B
More Feedback on What Consumers Want, Value and Expect from Us

Lisa from Virginia: "Any real estate agents I've used, have been friends. For the most part, ones who aren't my friends, I don't always trust as I've witnessed some vicious things. I value the time they're willing to spend with you and certainly the expertise that I lack. If I'm choosing an agent, I don't want someone pushy putting pressure on me to close a deal because all they see are dollar signs. I expect my agent to be honest and know the market."

Monty from California: "As an Investor and Builder I am doing fix and flips and we're selling on average two to three homes a month. I need a real estate agent on my team to handle all of our listings. I need an agent who is knowledgeable about financing and who has connections with the Lenders in our area because I want to make sure the contracts we have in place get funded at closing.

My agent has to be able to help us screen out buyers based on financial viability and my agent has to be able to work with the Appraisers during the appraisal process to make sure they have the market data and information on the house to make sure the appraisal process is a success. And my listing agent needs to have a strong web presence marketing our listings and a team of professionals for presenting the house with good pictures of the houses, video tours and staging.

Lastly I need a real estate agent who has an excellent reputation of getting deals closed and who is someone good to work with for the buyers agents. I don't have time to micro manage my agent so I trust they will do a good job and produce results. If the results are not there, then I get another agent."

Chris from North Carolina: "Knowledge of the area and homes for sale in the area and professionalism, just doing what they say they will do, being on time, prepared, knowledge of the homes they are showing. If I'm selling, it would be how they utilize more than a sign in my yard to market my home.

Past track record would help to identify ability. If I'm buying, knowledge and professionalism and hopefully a cheery/optimistic disposition since that's typically my wife and mine's mindset. Guidance on our local market, on the homes, on other transactions, mortgage lenders to consider, title companies, and appraisal partners. I would want them to show up with a readymade "team" of people that will also be professional and effective."

Bill from Boulder, Colorado: "I really only look for a few things in an agent so to answer your questions: I value honesty and experience. Barring experience, I value intelligence. I want someone who knows the area inside and out and knows how to leverage that to my advantage.

When choosing an agent, the most important thing to me is trust. I need to feel that the agent has my back and isn't just trying to make a fast buck. I expect my agent to kill for me. Seriously, the only thing I am looking for is a clone of me but with real estate knowledge when I am buying or selling a house. So I am mainly looking for someone who will always hold my interests first. Someone who actually cares that I will be happy even five years down the road. I want my agent to negotiate a better price when I buy a place and I want her to sell my place for what I ask for.

One negative experience I had with my condo purchase was that my agent failed to point out some of the disadvantages of my place before I bought it. I was just looking at the positives and I wish someone had pointed out some of the negatives even if it meant showing me more properties."

Chuck from Alabama: "I expect to be zealously represented. I expect honesty and integrity more than anything else. Be up front and honest with me if I'm selling a house. Take my calls when I call or return them in a reasonable amount of time. Know your market if I'm looking for a house and show me houses in the part of town I'm interested in and within my price range. If I tell you I can afford $250K, don't show me a $300K house unless you think I can get it for $250.

When I bought my house here where I live a few years ago, the agent kept taking us to other parts of town. We were in from out of state on a three day trip to find and bid on a house. She wasted our time the first day. We went online and actually found the house we ended up buying ourselves. Guess what? The house was listed by HER COMPANY and was smack dab in the middle of the area we told her we wanted to live in. That that agent got any of the commission on the sale of that house made me sick.

Once we made our offer, which was full price, and then it got worse. We ended up doing most of the leg work ourselves, dogging the closing and staying on top of it all. I flew down from out of state to close and when I got here the day before, found out some of the paperwork hadn't been done properly and the closing might have to be postponed. When I threatened to charge the real estate firm with my travel expenses if I had to come back, it all magically got done on time and we were able to close. It was a nightmare. I expect good follow up, staying on top of the deal, and just doing your job competently. But then, that's the key to doing any job well, isn't it?"

DeAnna from Boulder, Colorado: "Sincerity, authenticity and honesty. The person needs to be a genuine person and let their true personality shine through. If they are a no-nonsense, all business agent, fine. If they are more of a relaxed person and want to tell me details about their personal life kind of agent, I am fine with that. But to pretend to be something inauthentic because that's what they think the client wants is not a recipe for success.

I know a person online and he has his own business and he promotes himself through social media as a pretty heavy marketing tool. But he also posts a lot of political stuff which some people might say is a bad idea. But his theory is that he's going to be himself and clients that he's going work well with are naturally going to be drawn to that. And clients that he wouldn't work well with are going to be turned off—which is fine with him. Because if his primary concern is getting every single client; some of them he's going to end up hating and that won't end up working well for him or for the couple.

But I think it just comes back to being a genuine person. People can pick up on that, and that's how they begin to trust you and your input."

Laura from Wisconsin: "What I Look for: Someone who listens to what I want. Is honest and up front. Has a strategy. Takes care of all the details. Remembers what has been said. Tells the truth."

Tam Dalle Molle from Louisville, Colorado:
What do you value in a real estate agent? I value specific knowledge about the market the agent represents. Trends, comps, speculative information, typical inventory levels, historical appreciation, "good" neighborhoods vs. "questionable" ones, and that type of thing. I also value a strong sense of ethics. I want to feel I can fully trust that my agent has my best interest in mind, and is not motivated by his/her own financial benefit. There is nothing worse than feeling like your own real estate agent is pressuring you to buy something when you know in your gut it's not a good fit. I also like an agent who moves through the world in an ethical way—is not willing to cut corners or bend the rules in order to make a deal happen.

Strong knowledge of current laws with regard to inspections, appraisals, possible financing solutions, rental codes, etc. I rely on my real estate agent to keep me up to speed on how the laws have changed since my last transaction.

As in any business relationship, I like to surround myself with people who are genuinely fun to be around (my CPA and OB GYN are both hilarious, which makes my annual commitments to both of these folks less painful.) Purchasing real estate doesn't have to be a laugh a minute, but when pursuing real estate goals, I spend quite a bit of time with my agent, so I tend to pick people who have fun personalities. Who doesn't want to share a good laugh with their agent when someone posts pictures of their family room online that include people sitting on the couch and watching TV?

As an aside, I also value my agent's relationship with other professional specialists, plumbers, mortgage brokers, handymen, appraisers, electricians, inspectors, landscapers, etc. I have found that a reference from a respected agent is a strong reference indeed!

What is important to you in choosing an agent? And what do you expect from your real estate agent? (when buying or selling a home and even if you are an Investor)

Like I said above, I think trust is a key element. I need to know I am working with someone who is helping me to meet my goals, not his. I have found that many real estate agents fall into the "used car salesman" cliché, they talk smooth, they smell great, they wear fancy jewelry and drive a sweet car, but in the end, they are a salesperson. I don't want to work with a salesperson. I want to work with a partner. A guide, if you will, to help me navigate through the jungle of a real estate transaction. I don't want to feel like my agent looks at me and sees the potential dollars he can earn from me. I am looking for someone who genuinely likes helping people find what they are looking for.

And lastly from my real estate agent, I expect honesty, patience, a good sense of humor, and the ability to work on my behalf in an ethical way."

Kym from North Carolina: "We've used the same agent twice and what we value in her is: Her HONEST opinion of the current situation of the home we are considering and the future investment of it. Are they going to a four lane highway where the nice country road is now next to the house? We wanted someone who wasn't just going to tell us what we wanted to hear. We needed her knowledge of the school systems as we didn't have school aged kids when we bought our first two houses. We valued her network of inspectors and fix-it people to get a real opinion on what needed to be done to a home and how much it would cost to fix it. We chose her based on recommendations from friends."

Scot from Virginia: "What I value most in a real estate agent is communication. When selling my house I expect open and honest communication during the discussion of price setting, tell me the truth based on comparables, and then communicate with me via email or whatever means is most convenient, buyer activity on a weekly basis. In addition to this, follow up for comments from agents who have shown the house periodically is also extremely helpful."

Blonnie from Virginia: "To answer your question, I suppose that I expect the real estate agent to have our backs, not to shove something down our throats that we don't want. I'm a big proponent of honesty. If there is a problem with a property, I want to know about it."

Michael from Boulder, Colorado:

What do you value in a real estate agent? Two main thoughts here, partly dependent on market conditions and my objectives: integrity and access. Integrity is always important, because I expect to spend a lot of time with the agent and I don't want to spend time with someone I don't respect. Access was a priority in two situations, when I was trying to buy during tight/fast market conditions, and when I was trying to buy good building lots (not in a subdivision)—all told I've bought 4 vacant lots in CO and sold 3 as lots, the 4th after building a home on it. In the first case, access meant working with an agent that was part of a larger operation, so they were aware of upcoming listings that I could possibly preview and make offers on before they appeared in MLS. In the latter case, it was better to have an agent with more of a niche focus.

What is important to you in choosing an agent? Confidence that they will work their butt off for my interests, and being knowledgeable about important features in that market segment. As a negative example, I used a friend to help secure some commercial space when we decided to open some businesses. While they worked hard with me and the landlord to get some favorable lease clauses, we still ended up with a much higher lease rate than we should have paid. As a positive example, this same friend was insistent on me hiring a good structural engineer to review the property we bought in Superior, and it saved us considerable future distress by finding problems and getting the seller to make some major repairs to the foundation and the drainage before we'd close.

And what do you expect from your real estate agent? A buyer's agent will be able to absorb what we are really looking for after 5-10 showings of candidate properties, so they don't waste our time putting junk in front of us when we are looking. They will help us evaluate neighborhoods as well as specific properties, and point out factors both positive and negative that we may have overlooked. They will help us negotiate the most favorable terms for us on the purchase without unreasonably penalizing the seller.

A seller's agent will actively, not passively, market out listing. They will help us understand how best to prepare/position our home so that it shows favorably and commands a reasonable price. They will take most of our concerns away during the closing process by ensuring we know what is expected of us with plenty of lead time.

Appendix C
Random Tips

1) **Pareto Principle**

I highly recommend you study this and see how it applies to being a real estate agent. The Pareto Principle is also known as the 80-20 rule.

Twenty percent of the real estate agents generate eighty percent of the sales. And conversely, eighty percent of the real estate agents generate twenty percent of the sales. Which category do you want to be in? Of course, you want to be in the top twenty percent. Over time, you are going to identify which agents in your market are in the top twenty percent. Learn from them, watch what they do, and try to incorporate their methods and strategies into your business. You will also identify which agents are in the eighty percent and should try to avoid what they do.

Twenty percent of your clients represent eighty percent of your commissions. You need all the clients you can get in your early years, but remember that some clients will be more profitable to you than others.

Twenty percent of the real estate companies are generating eighty percent of the sales. When you are considering where to work, I suggest you take this into account. Ideally, you want to work for a company that is a "player" in your local market.

2) **Post-Sell**

This is a sales strategy I learned very early in my sales career. Buyer's remorse always sets in after a buyer or seller agrees to a contract. It's your job to post-sell to your clients so they continue to feel that they made the right decision. Our clients are looking to us for reassurance a lot of times, and you need to be aware of this and help them.

The next day you're talking to your buyer after the contract has been agreed to, you can say the following: "I am very happy for you, this is a great house for you." "We finally found the right house." "Congrats again." Don't be too strong in your post-selling because there's a good possibility the contract could fall apart as a result of the inspection or appraisal process.

Use the same strategy with your seller. "That's great, does it feel good to have your house under contract?" "Congrats again on getting under contract, they look like solid buyers." Just keep it simple, but keep reminding them that they made the right decision and that they should be excited. With sellers it can be tough, depending on the specifics of the deal, because you don't want to post-sell too much if the sellers had to accept a really low price, or if it's a short sale.

Use your best judgment when post-selling your clients. Just a little bit of post-selling will go a long way.

3) Build Your Service Contacts

You are a resource for your clients, so you need to build a contact list of service providers in the area. Examples are:

Mortgage Lenders (I like to refer at least two local lenders I know who do a good job).

Home Inspectors (refer at least two reputable inspection companies to your clients).

Electricians, Plumbers, Roofers, Painters, Carpet and Tile, Hardwood Floor, Handymen, Concrete Repair, Deck Repair, Building Contractors, Lawyers, Title Companies, CPA's, Radon Mitigation Companies, Pest Control, and any other service or trades people related to a house.

Some real estate agents leverage their recommendation of their service contacts with the companies in order to attain real estate referrals from the service companies. Go back and reread Liz Caraway's story in Appendix A where she talks about creating a "Service Provider Directory" and the strategy she uses.

4) Business Plan

Do you have to do this? I hate business plans; there, I said it. I feel much better now. I have to confess, I have never done a business plan in my life. I am just not wired that way. I am a salesperson first and will always be one. I am not an engineer. I have always felt that things are going to work out for me because I am good at what I do, and I believe in my abilities to close deals and be successful. I don't believe in building spreadsheet models for my business. My wife hates this about me because she wants me to know all of my costs and how much money I need to be profitable. Guess what, she's an engineer. I have a goal in mind every year for my business for how much I want to earn in commissions and it has turned out well for me.

You are welcome to do a business plan, but just be careful about wasting too much time and energy on it. It's easy for me because I try to spend as little money as possible on my marketing efforts.

5) You're a Sales Target for Vendors

Here is a list of stuff that people will try to sell to you: wall calendars, refrigerator magnet business cards, refrigerator magnets with your picture on it, fancy business cards with your picture on it, postcards services, newsletter services, letter writing services, custom pens, custom water bottles, notepads, desk calendars, notebooks, custom tote bags, custom coffee cups, custom key chains, custom umbrellas, custom picnic blankets, custom golf balls, custom baseball caps, custom wine stoppers, custom letter openers, custom calculators, custom lip balm, custom ice cream scoopers, custom sports bags, custom snug fleece blankets, custom can openers, custom clips for paper, and the list could go on and on. I think you get the idea.

People will try to sell you all kinds of products to increase your business and generate more leads. Don't fall for any of them. A ton of people and companies make a living selling their "junk" to real estate agents. Don't fall for any of these get-rich-quick schemes. My rule of thumb is: If it sounds too good to be true, then don't buy it.

Be prepared for a lot of phone calls to your office and cell phone from these companies. I get calls all the time on my cell phone. One that I often get comes from area code "925" and it's a recorded message stating, "we have real-time buyers in your area" and it's at this point that I hang up. Be very careful about any of these lead generation companies. They are never very clear about what the cost is to you. They might say there's only a startup fee between $50 and $100, and then they are not clear after that what happens; most likely there's a back-end referral fee of 25% to 30% of your commission. Just don't take any of these calls when they call you, and believe me you will get them, especially if you are just starting out.

6) Dual Income Couples

In today's economy, dual income couples are more successful and have less stress in their lives. This is one of the dirty little secrets in real estate that most agents do not talk about. Your spouse has their own career separate from yours, and they make an income that is not dependent on your business. Regardless of being a real estate agent or not, most couples nowadays are dual income; it's just how most people live now. My wife is a software engineer, and she gets a steady paycheck which offsets the irregular nature of my commissions. The other advantage to this structure is that we have health insurance through my wife's company, since I do not have access to any company-paid healthcare through my real estate company.

7) Don't Be Something You're Not

Beware of trying to wear too many hats with your clients! It's best to focus on your area of expertise in a real estate transaction and not to overstep your boundaries. You are a real estate agent, not a lender, not a home inspector, not a building contractor, not a title representative, and not a lawyer. When you get heavily involved with your clients, you might be tempted to do whatever you can to keep the deal together. Resist the temptation! In the best-case scenario, it will come back to bite you, reflect negatively on you, and weaken your value to your clients. Worst case, you will be involved in a lawsuit for misrepresenting your levels of expertise. So don't do it! Here are some ways I help my clients avoid confusion about where I can and cannot help them.

- I am a real estate agent, not a lender. Whenever I get questions on rates or loan terms, I always direct my clients to talk with their lender. If they are not working with one yet or their lender is not forthcoming with information, I refer them to a few lenders I know who do a good job and whom I trust. I don't have the time, expertise or desire to follow all of the loan rates for the different loan products available. Once we are under contract, I always refer all lender and loan issues to the lender who is handling the loan.

- I am a real estate agent, not a home inspector. We all know the inspection phase can be the riskiest part of the process. This is where deals fall apart, and we may be tempted to answer questions or give our opinion about how big of an issue a particular inspection finding is. Again, a strong word of caution here is to resist temptation! Many real estate offices now have formal office policies against their real estate agents attending home inspections, and for good reason. Real Estate Agent Magazine has recently covered several court rulings against real estate agents who were sued by their buyers for making inaccurate statements about an inspection report. It's best to let the home inspector and buyer discuss these issues themselves and let the buyer decide how they want to proceed. I limit my advice and counsel to my experience with other homes in the neighborhood.

- I am a real estate agent, not a building contractor. Clients will often ask my opinion of issues related to home construction. Unless I have exact knowledge of the construction of the building in question, it's best to defer these kinds of questions to a builder or contractor.

- I am a real estate agent, not a title representative. As a result of the contract process, there is a ton of paperwork generated from the title company handling the closing. If my client has any questions related to the title work, I refer them to the title company. Again, I probably could answer many of these questions but it's best not to.

- I am a real estate agent, not a lawyer. This is a fine line since, as real estate agents, we are executing contracts and legal documents, yet we are not lawyers. When my clients ask for legal advice or counsel beyond my knowledge of standard real estate contracts and forms, I tell them that they should contact a lawyer. For example, I had a listing where there was a boundary dispute between one of the neighbors and my seller. My seller had a lawyer prepare and send a letter to the neighbor that outlined the issues. The neighbor agreed and took steps not to encroach on my seller's property as a result of this letter. If my seller had asked me to draft such a letter, I would not have been qualified to do so, nor to give legal advice on the matter.

As a professional salesperson, you need to become an expert in managing client expectations. You can unknowingly set improper expectations with your clients and set yourself up to fail just by talking about areas that are outside of your domain as a real estate agent. You may have a strong opinion on the subject or even a good answer, but you should still refer these questions to the real experts. I do know a lot of real estate agents who are also builders, lenders, or lawyers, but most of us are not. So stick to what you know, wear your real estate agent hat, and don't discuss or set expectations on issues that could end up hurting your clients.

8) Strengths as an Individual Real Estate Agent

As an individual real estate agent, you provide a much more personable and hands-on experience for your clients than a Team, Limited Service, or Entry Only real estate agent ever could. You provide a consistent presence from the very first meeting through the closing. The continuity and personal attention you offer is reassuring and important to clients who expect a high level of service when buying or selling their home. In some team real estate agent business models, the lead real estate agent has a minimal client-facing role. His or her staff and team work with the clients once the lead real estate agent signs them up. I have talked with some people who were disappointed with this model. They got to know and were sold on the team's services by the lead real estate agent in an initial meeting, but did not see him or her again until their final meeting at the closing table. Being handed off to other members of the team made them feel lower priority. Continuity and attention to detail is critical to buyers and sellers. They expect not to have to re-explain their situation every time they talk to you.

Even as a real estate agent, calling into a team real estate agent's office I get frustrated with the level of service. If I'm calling to ask about one of their listings, I invariably end up talking to a staff person who is not a real estate agent. When I ask questions about the property, they do the best they can to answer, even though I can tell they have never seen the property. My questions go unanswered and I have to work ten times harder just to get the basic information I need. I can only imagine how frustrating this is for buyers and sellers.

As an individual real estate agent, you are able to provide greater responsiveness and flexibility because you know your clients' wants and needs personally. If it's important to schedule a same-day showing, you do it because you have that personal relationship with your clients. You know their expectations, you work hard to follow through and give them the results they want and need, and your reputation—nobody else's—is on the line.

Going the Extra Mile

Your personal relationship with your clients often gives you the opportunity to go the extra mile for them. This is the personal touch that no other real estate agent business model can replicate and one of the strengths you should capitalize on as an individual real estate agent. Think about ways you could go the extra mile for your existing customers. For example, when touring homes with buyers I always make it a point to drive them around the neighborhood they are interested in, show them the downtown area, and point out parks, city services, and other notable spots I know they would like to see. This takes little to no time and helps "sell" a client on both the area and my knowledge and expertise as a real estate agent. When your client has a special need or a problem comes up, as an individual real estate agent you have the opportunity to make a fast decision and take care of their issue immediately. This builds trust, puts you in a power position, and gets you clients and referrals for life.

I have done a lot of unusual things for my clients over the years in keeping with my "go the extra mile" philosophy. Once, I attended an Inspection Review for my clients because they were out of town. I took a ton of pictures for them and reviewed the inspection with the home inspector. This is not something I would normally do, but these clients really had no other option. The extra time I spent on this was worth it because the inspection process went smoothly and we closed on the house within the next two weeks.

Another time I kept an eye on a house for some buyers after their closing. Again, they were new to the area and needed someone they trusted to monitor the house until they moved in. I even snow shoveled their driveway and sidewalk a couple of times. This paid off for me because my clients wrote me a very positive testimonial to use on my website and referred me to a new client. Going the extra mile will pay off for you, too.

Being an Educator and Listener

Since you are a professional individual real estate agent, you have the ability to offer a much more pleasant sales experience for your clients, which will always pay off for you. Selling is not telling, so it's your responsibility to educate your clients during the process rather than just showing them the properties they want to see. The old model of promoting and pushing properties does not work anymore. Selling your own value and expertise, on the other hand, is an approach your clients will appreciate. Educate your clients on their options, since the best decision is an informed decision, and let them make their own choice.

As an individual real estate agent, you are able to focus on truly listening to what your client wants and needs. Listening is a skill that all successful professional sales-people have when helping their clients. An inexperienced and nervous salesperson is always talking when they should be listening. The real estate agent who talks more than their client will alienate him or her and fail to develop a strong relationship. So actively listen to your clients and do what they ask. Just take the time to listen and your client will tell you all of their needs, concerns, and what is important to them. When you remember your client's wants and needs, you waste less of your time and theirs. For example, if a buyer wants you to show her properties in a certain area and price range, do what she asks. If you show her houses outside of her scope, you will risk upsetting her or making her feel that you did not listen. Once you demonstrate that you fully understand her wants and needs, she will be loyal to you and value your expert opinion even more.

The Value of Patience and Honesty
Your level of patience is also a valuable skill that can set you apart with your clients. This sounds simple, but it can be difficult for us as salespeople, since our income is affected by every closing. It's not important how long the sales cycle takes, but that you produce results for your clients and get them to a successful closing. So if your seller wants to wait until a higher priced offer comes in, you respect their decision. If your buyer is lukewarm about a house and wants to wait until a more suitable one comes on the market, you continue to help them with their search. Pushing clients into making decisions they really don't want to make will inevitably damage your relationship with them. Sellers and buyers value and appreciate the patience their real estate agent shows, and never want to feel they have been manipulated or pushed into making a decision.

Your level of honesty with your clients is also an area where you can shine. As salespeople we all value honesty, but one of our biggest hurdles is how to reconcile the honesty we know we should have with the "shark principle" we explored earlier. We may fear that being brutally honest in response to some questions will be a deal-killer. Due to the level of intimacy we have built with our client, we also may be aware that they do not understand a particular issue, so we know we can answer their question in any number of ways. This is dangerous territory and can either make or break your reputation as a real estate agent.

It is my strong opinion that you should always answer these potentially deal-breaking questions with the utmost candor and honesty. This is tough, but besides being the right thing to do, it will always pay off for you. As we have discussed before, helping your clients get what they want and need helps *you* get what you want and need! I always use this honest approach, and will continue to do so, because my clients appreciate and value my honesty. When we do get to a point where my response will seal the deal for my clients, they trust my response even more since I have earned their trust by always being honest with them. This is also a personally gratifying and satisfying way to do business, and I promise you will enjoy your professional life more if your policy is always honesty.

Finally, your focus on a niche or specialty area will set you apart from the other business models, and other individual real estate agents. Prospective clients will value and respect you more because you have expertise in an area of interest to them. Before you even meet these clients, they already see you as sharing an interest or something in common with them, and are envisioning ways you can help them with their unique situation. Your experience allows you to deliver on these expectations. You are able to identify, understand, and anticipate niche clients' needs much more fully than other real estate agents do, and as a result, the service you deliver to them will be unmatched.

Make sure to promote your competitive advantages to every prospective client you come in contact with. Since you are a professional, you never speak badly about your competition, but you can always promote your strengths. Your website and all of your marketing collateral reflect your strengths so prospective clients are aware of what sets you apart.

9) Ride out the Highs and Lows of Each Client
There is no doubt that our jobs as real estate agents can be stressful. Do any of these situations sound familiar to you?

1. You have a listing that has been on the market for eight months, and you are finally under contract after four lowball offers. At the inspection phase, the contract falls apart because the buyer is being hard-nosed, asking for repairs and credits. Your client, the seller, feels they have already given in a lot on the price. You try the best you can, but the contract is terminated per the inspection.

2. You have been touring homes for four months and you have viewed over 50 homes with your buyers. They are very picky and have specific criteria for their new home. It's a challenge to find them the right home in the right city and neighborhood to meet their needs, but you stick to it because they are committed to you as their real estate agent, and your qualifying questions revealed that they have the means and motivation to make a decision soon. Then the buyers tell you they have decided to stop looking this year and they want to wait until next summer to start looking again.

3. You are ten days away from a closing, and you get a phone call from your buyer telling you they are considering backing out of the contract. The buyer feels things at work are very shaky, there has been talk of layoffs, and he feels he may be next. You have spent a lot of time with this buyer, and this is the third contract for purchase you have entered into with him since the first two contracts did not come together. You have viewed close to 40 homes together over two months in three different cities. The house in question is a perfect fit for your

buyer; it has everything they are looking for in a house. But given these new financial concerns, you don't know if you are going to make it to the closing.

How do you deal with these situations? These are the tough times that all real estate agents face when working with their clients. It's late at night and you can't sleep because a lot is at stake. I think the hardest part of being in sales is dealing with these unknowns. Days go by when you don't know whether or not you will make it to the closing, and your fate and the fate of your clients hangs in the balance. This weighs on you day and night and can create a lot of stress.

As real estate agents and salespeople, we have all been up late at night worrying about our deals and not being able to sleep. It's just a part of our business that will always be there. The key is how you deal with it, and how you respond going forward. Mentally, you have to be strong. You can insert all of the sports analogies or motivational quotes you want about tough times; we've heard them all before. I'd like to give you some real coping skills for getting you through the long, dark nights we all face.

I remember when I was managing my sales team at Rogue Wave Software years ago, and how hard it was on some of my sales reps when they lost a deal. They took it so personally! One of the ways I tried to help them, as a manager, was to explain that they needed to "focus on what they could control." If they lost a deal due to something they could not control, they shouldn't feel bad. Things happen all the time that we can't control. That's how life is. So the next time things go badly for you in your business as a real estate agent, just remember that if it's outside of your control, then there is nothing you can do about it. Stop second-guessing yourself. You are often your own toughest critic; so let the bad feelings go when a situation is out of your control. Stop thinking about it and move on. We don't realize how much damage these negative thoughts can have over time. Be in control of your thoughts and break out of the negativity. Stop fixating on a deal that went badly. There will always be another deal. Move on mentally so you can help someone else get to their closing.

Another way to cope with lost deals is to maintain a good pipeline reporting system or sales forecast like I discussed before. Whenever I lose a client or a contract is terminated, I update my pipeline spreadsheet and look at my deals again. This helps me focus on what it will take to reach my commission goal. I always factor in a certain percentage of losses in my forecast. Of course I always work towards closing all buyers and listings, but the reality is that unknowns are always part of the equation. Your forecast spreadsheet ensures that you don't live in the world of hope, but in the world of reality. By being realistic when calculating my pipeline, I do the best I can to have as many active and future clients as "insurance" against the deals I do end up losing. This is how sales is; you can't close all of your deals. As you get more practical about updating your forecast and reviewing it regularly, especially when you lose a deal due to unforeseen circumstances, you will find yourself getting stronger and more resilient.

Losing contracts or clients can have positive consequences. I personally get a rush of energy to contact my sphere, do more networking, and call, email, or visit some of my contacts after I lose a contract. This burst of focus allows me to fill the top of my sales pipeline with leads that will generate more business for the future. It's a good release for me, and a very productive stress management tool. It always makes me feel better because it distracts me from what happened, my activities are worthwhile, and when I am done, I can once again look to the positives in my future instead of dwelling on the past. If you try this strategy, be very mindful of your mood and stay positive.

You should have a handful of friends and contacts that you can have lunch with who will pick up your spirits. Having lunch with someone who inspires you is a great idea when you lose a contract or client. There's no need to discuss your problems at the lunch. Just enjoy their company and have fun.

My last strategy for dealing with the tough times is to always remember the good times and the great reasons I have for being in this business. I think of all the people I have helped over the years. I think of the friendships I have developed with my clients and re-read my testimonials. I remember the good feelings I had with each client once we made it to the closing table, and how happy everyone was once the transaction was complete. I remember how much each client appreciated me and thanked me for my work. The joy and satisfaction I get from helping each client keeps me moving forward so I can help more clients in the future. Remember not to get too caught up in the negative parts of your job, and always remember the "high" that you get every time you help a client.

When you are having success, take the time to truly enjoy it. Pat yourself on the back and feel good about what you have accomplished, but remember that your work is not yet done. After a successful closing, I always make it a point to get in touch with clients who are on the fence about getting started because my confidence is at its peak. I learned this tactic from my days of selling in high tech. The best time to call your most challenging prospect is right after a sale, because your confidence and self-esteem are at an all-time high. You are feeling great about yourself after a sale, and this can't help but translate into positive things, even for your most difficult case. So don't hesitate, discipline yourself to pick up the phone and call them right after you walk out of a closing!

As real estate agents, we need to be client-focused rather than deal-focused. This section is not called "Ride Out the Highs and Lows of Each Deal" because we usually have to go through multiple contracts with a client before getting to a successful closing. By concentrating on riding out the highs and lows of each client, the client's needs rather than the deal come first. Always remember that you work for the client, not the deal. Contracts are terminated all the time as a part of the sales process, so don't get too disappointed when this happens. You will do your best to make sure the next contract you get with that client makes it to the closing. Your focus should always be on the future.

I disagree with the popular saying that "problems equal opportunity." I have heard this so many times over the years from the motivational speakers. The reality is that you do have challenges and problems which come up with clients, and a real problem is something you have to face. How you overcome your problems and lost sales will be the true test of your professionalism. In the long run, practicing positive responses to these challenges will pay off because you will gain more experience and strength as a result.

10) Look Within, Not Without
I have been a professional salesperson for many years, and I have bought and read a ton of sales books, sales and motivational audio tapes, attended sales and motivational seminars, formal company sales training, and I have spent thousands of dollars. What was I looking for? A sure-fire way to be successful, earn more money, be happier, be healthier? What was I seeking? I ask myself these questions today, and I think I was looking for an easy way to be successful. Over time, I realized the answer I was seeking was within me. I just needed to do the work, focus on what is important, and do the best I can every day. I wasted tons of money and time searching for something that never existed. I wish someone had pulled me aside and told me what I know now; there are no shortcuts in life.

I give you my perspective on personal development because we, as real estate agents, are bombarded constantly by people trying to sell us stuff: training programs, coaching and mentoring programs, contact management systems, software programs, marketing paraphernalia, guaranteed selling systems, lead generation systems, leads, and every other imaginable thing. I absolutely despise the people who are trying to scam real estate agents with their high priced seminars and programs. You know exactly what I am talking about because we all get tons of junk mail, spam emails, and phone calls to our office and cell phones. How do they find us? It's just crazy how much we are targeted as real estate agents. They keep on us because they know a good percentage of real estate agents will buy these programs. Sadly, in my opinion, and based on my experience, 95 percent of these programs will not help your business. So who wins here? The vendors certainly do, not the real estate agents.

Take a good look at the real estate industry magazines you get. Most of the pages are just ads trying to sell to us. Nowadays, I pitch most of these magazines into our recycle bin at the office without opening them up. I am really disappointed in the way we are targeted so much by others within our industry.

Have you noticed how many national real estate trainers and coaches there are in our industry? How many of these trainers and coaches are active real estate agents?

I always wonder what these folks can offer if they have not been active as a real estate agent in a long time. Our market has changed so much since the 1980s. The last ten years alone have seen a tremendous amount of change. It just seems to me that these trainers do a really good job of selling their training and coaching programs, but is their content relevant? Do they add value to us as real estate agents, and help us with our everyday business? Maybe some do, but it's something to think hard about the next time you are writing them a check.

There are of course a lot of motivational speakers making the circuit throughout the real estate industry. Do you really need someone to motivate you to do your job? If you are a professional, then I don't think you do. Don't waste your time and money on these programs. Look within yourself for the motivation and the inspiration you already have because you are good at what you do and you care about your clients.

Over time, I have been approached to participate in local Chamber of Commerce meetings, networking groups, and brown bag meetings. I do not attend because I believe they are a complete waste of time. Cut these "non-selling" activities out of your schedule and focus on your business. These networking opportunities are all thinly disguised efforts to sell products and services. This does not work for us as real estate agents. No one in these groups is going to make the decision to use you as their real estate agent on the basis of your interactions with them there.

What is valuable is spending time with other real estate agents who are successful and learning from them. It's also important to be around other successful people outside of our profession. This can be both inspiring and instructive, as we learn new strategies that we can implement or translate as they apply to real estate. Believe in yourself, stick to what you know, and just do the work. You don't need any charlatan selling a self-help program to know what you should do. How many of these individuals are doing what you do each day as a real estate agent? I am a real estate agent just like you, and I am not guaranteeing a million dollar payoff. I am giving you ideas which will help you earn a living and enjoy a lifetime as a real estate agent.

11) What is purposely not in this book?
I am not a big believer in scripts and forcing a conversation based on a script. So I have purposely not included any scripts as they relate to: prospecting, listing presentations, buyer counseling presentations, and "How's the Market?" scripts.

I was forced to use scripts in my first few sales jobs and I always found them to be forced and unnatural. Today's consumers are well informed and knowledgeable, so they will be able to see through the scripts and forced conversations.

The best way to address this as you start out is to learn the material and get comfortable with it, and then focus on what your motivation is. The book **The One Minute Salesperson** applies here; it states, "your selling purpose is to help other people get what they want and need and in return you will receive what you want and need."

Appendix D
Inspirational Movies

When you get run down and need a lift, consider watching one of these movies.

Breaking Away
Rocky (the first one)
Rudy
Hoosiers
The Lives of Others
The Karate Kid (original with Pat Morita)
Three O'clock High
Cinderella Man
Working Girl
The Shawshank Redemption
Dave
Remember the Titans
The Blind Side
Secretariat
Seabiscuit
Facing the Giants
Erin Brockovich
The Champ
Jerry Maguire

Thanks to Angie L. Ferriera for some of these movie suggestions.

About The Author:

Mario Jannatpour is currently an active Realtor and works for RE/MAX Alliance in Louisville, Colorado.

Mario has studied the sales profession intensely since 1986. From his early days in sales, he has listened to audio tape series on sales and personal development, read sales books, attended sales seminars, and participated in formal sales training. Mario has been successful as a Sales Representative, in Sales Management and now as a Realtor. In this book, Mario has brought together the best of what he has learned and practiced over the years and how it relates to real estate. Mario has been a Realtor since 2002, and is still actively helping his clients buy and sell homes. He and his wife, Smitha, and their two daughters, Ria and Puja, live in Louisville, Colorado.

Message From The Author:

Thanks so much for buying my book. Check out the Honest Real Estate Agent Video Series available on Amazon. Good luck in your new career.